DEDICATED
TO
MY FATHER AND MOTHER

FOREWORD

by

Bishop Paul B. Kern

PREACHING is an art. In the highest reaches of his pulpit ministration the preacher is an artist. He must use imagination and thought and feeling and will to create his final impression upon the canvas of men's minds and hearts. He can wrongly mix his colors, mishandle his perspective, and leave his whole picture dull and flat. To be a real preacher is the work of a life-time and the wise man calls to his assistance the aid of every art and device that will make his message more compelling and effective.

Among the first requisites of a sermon is that it shall be interesting. People are seldom moved to higher goals by words that are dull and disorderly. To grip the attention opens the door to the will. It is not sufficient to say words that are true; they must be said so that those who hear will rise up and become doers of the word. Most people are picture-minded. In the graphic lives of a word picture they see reality and life and the image of it is carried back into the walks of common life. Jesus, the flawless Teacher, talked to his followers in parables. These were pictures, "illustrations" as we say. Wise is the preacher who has mastered that art and knows how to open windows into truth and throw on the canvas of the mind unforgettable images that hold within their phrases the truths of eternal life.

The author of this timely volume sat in the classroom with me and gave promise then of the fine contribution which he has been making to the cause of good preaching in America. In this volume he blazes a trail into a new field and does it so well that one finds within these pages all that he needs to show him the road into the effective handling of homiletic material. This book ought to contribute very positively to better preaching and such an offering of help will be quickly accepted by the eager, growing preacher and appreciated by the congregation that sits under his pulpit messages.

DURHAM, N. C.

CONTENTS

9

INTRODUCTION

I HAPPENED upon a little treatise written nearly a hundred years ago by Dr. Dowling, and I marvel that the following statement is as true today as when he wrote it. "I have selected a subject," he said, "upon which comparatively little (in my estimation, far too little) is said in the works, which it has been my lot to examine, on Homiletics, Rhetoric, or Eloquence. And often has it been to me a matter of surprise that, in the textbooks on these subjects, hundreds of pages are sometimes occupied with instructions relative to voice and manner and action; or to argument and method and style—while the subject of illustration, if alluded to at all, is frequently dismissed with barely a passing remark." [1]

It has been my privilege to read practically everything that has been written concerning illustrating sermons, and yet that is not very much. Books on preaching only contain from a few paragraphs to a single chapter. One book has two chapters.[2] Of course there are many collections and encyclopedias of stories and anecdotes, but nowhere is there a discussion of the art and method of illustrating a sermon or a speech.

For my own preaching I needed to know where illustrations were found, how they were made, and how they could be used. During the past several years I have tried to find the art that lay behind the finest illustrations and the best

[1] Notes will be found at end of book, beginning on page 261.

pulpit illustrators. The following chapters are an effort to give to my brethren in the ministry the results of these investigations. This is not a collection of illustrations, although some of the choicest and most carefully selected modern ones are contained in it. It is an effort to discover how the best preachers work and make their illustrations, and the principles which, if followed, would enable anyone to become a master of pulpit illustration. I have not attained (how well I know it), but I am certain that if the methods suggested in these pages were followed, my sermons would become more useful. It is my hope that out of the principles suggested ministers may develop their preaching, and serve better their congregations and our Lord.

Since the purpose of the book is to discover the underlying principles and methods of successfully illustrating sermons, the reader will discover that certain types of illustrations, such as "poetry," "fiction," etc., will recur, although with different emphasis, at several points in the discussion.

I am greatly indebted to many friends who have given valuable advice and helpful criticism in the preparation of the manuscript. In the early stages Dr. Paul W. Quillian, pastor of First Methodist Church, Houston, made many useful and luminous suggestions. Bishop Paul B. Kern, my seminary teacher of homiletics; Dr. Ivan Lee Holt, pastor of St. John's Methodist Church, St. Louis; Dr. C. Wesley Webdell, presiding elder of the St. Louis District; Dr. Luther E. Todd, for many years a successful pastor and now with the Board of Finance of the Methodist Episcopal Church, South;

INTRODUCTION

Dr. W. W. Parker, President of Southeast Missouri Teachers' College, and my wife have read the manuscript and have offered valuable comment. Some of the younger men in the ministry have been stimulating as they have discussed their particular needs in sermon preparation. To these and others I am grateful for assistance and counsel.

Centenary Methodist Church,   DAWSON C. BRYAN.
St. Louis, Missouri.

I

PREACHING IN WHICH PEOPLE SEE

No preacher need be uninteresting. No sermon need be dull. It is possible for every minister's preaching to throb with animation and compelling interest.

And yet much preaching moves with leaden feet to an unsought goal of weary listeners and unmoved hearts. It was not so with Jesus. The people heard him gladly, because he made plain the truth of his message by using a picture language which they could understand.

A dull preacher of a past generation said to his congregation, "If you cannot keep awake without it, when you feel drowsy, why don't you take a pinch of snuff?" At the close of the service one of his hearers gave this shrewd but good-natured reply: "I think the snuff should be put into the sermons."

The impotence of many modern sermons is not that they are too concerned with facts but that there is far too little illumination of the facts. The mind is informed, but the heart and will are not touched. It is not great or even passable preaching until the mind is persuaded, the feelings are aroused, and conduct is intensified or changed. Emotions are stirred and decisions made not so much through argument as through visual realization.

Ruskin said, "The greatest thing a human soul ever does in this world is to *see* something, and tell what he *saw* in a plain way. Hundreds of people can talk for one who thinks, but thousands can think for one who can see. To see clearly is poetry, prophecy, religion—all in one." [1] Of many preachers in this practical-minded generation it might be spoken: "One thing thou lackest—imagination."

WINDOWS OF LIGHT

Bishop Paul B. Kern once said to a class in preaching: "The window shades are drawn and the room is dark. One shade is lifted and light streams in. Another shade is raised and through that window more light comes in. The third shade is lifted and the room is completely flooded with sunshine. This, my young friends, is what illustrations will do to your sermons. But there is one consideration you must bear in mind; after the room is well lighted, the added effect of one or two more windows means little or nothing, except glare."

Into the argument and thought of the sermon come the illustrations as light through windows. They add luster, variety, illumination. One illustration, how much it is needed! Another adds more light, and perhaps another, but after the room is well lighted other windows are superfluous. Too many illustrations cheapen the sermon.

PREACHING IN WHICH PEOPLE SEE

We shall concern ourselves in the following discussion with one of the most necessary arts of the ministry: making windows in sermons.

THE MOVING PICTURE MIND

The necessity of illuminating the sermon properly is found in the mental attitude of the people. Whether we like it or not most of us preach to the "moving picture mind." It is the mind accustomed to images, pictures, scenes, rapidly moving. It certainly is not accustomed to deep thinking or long, sustained argument. Current magazines, billboards, novels, drama, rapid transit, all add to this popular method of visual thinking. We as ministers may not approve of the daily fare of the people; we may regret their inability to pursue abstract logic; we may wish them to prefer theoretical reasoning. But, whatever our wishes, we must recognize that they regard thinking which is not imaginative and concrete as dull and uninteresting. They often complain, "He is preaching over our heads," when they really mean, "His message is heavy and colorless." A college professor, a member of a cultured congregation, once said to his pastor, "Your sermons are interesting, full of illustrations, and the people see."

As ministers we are not to take our pattern from the cinema, yet we cannot afford to overlook the fact that our congregations, or the people we wish would come to hear us, do see pictorially. Dr. Howard Chandler Robbins, formerly Dean of the Cathedral of St. John the Divine, New York City, epitomizes a conclusion drawn from years of preaching when

17

he says, "I am more and more convinced that the appeal to the ordinary congregation is through 'eye-gate' rather than through 'ear-gate.' People think in pictures, and remember parables." [2]

PICTURES STICK

Psychologists continually remind us that this generation is visually minded. People are not good listeners. What they receive comes largely through the eye, particularly through reading and the daily panorama. The radio may be turning people back toward a greater use of their ears, but this is doubtful, since most of the programs still consist of songs, drama, and advertising, with practically no requirements for sustained thinking. College students have learned to study with the radio "blah-blahing"; housewives do their work to its popular tunes, without much listening, and Dad in the evening is soothed by it as he peruses the daily paper. Radio still has an unfinished task if it is to change us from picture-thinking to ear-thinking.

The preacher will do well to take this visual-mindedness for what it is worth and paint pictures which will be converted in the listener's mind into unforgettable mental images. That, of course, is just what happens in realistic preaching. How often do people remember abstract truth expressed in a sermon as compared to the illustrations or events described?

I remember clearly a sermon I heard on immortality when just a boy, or rather I remember an illustration which the preacher used. What else he said I do not now recall, but that picture which he presented greatly strengthened my youthful conviction of the continuation of life beyond the grave. He concluded that morning by saying:

"A little boy was playing in the sands along the seashore. He was building a city in the sand. He laid out the streets, built the houses, stores, banks, churches, and homes. And with a childish fancy he placed around his modern community an ancient city wall. Outside the wall he laid out highways and roads, farms and farmhouses. All afternoon he worked, building his city. He did not notice that the sun was setting, that the clouds were gathering, that the wind was growing chill. He was too busy with his city. He did not notice that the tide was coming in, the waves mounting higher and higher, until one wave, mightier than the rest, came sweeping in about him, washing away his houses and his lands, his city and his farms. In terror the little child ran back against the cliff, alone and afraid.

"But above him on the cliff sat his older brother. He had seen it all. He had watched his younger brother play as once he had played in the sands; he had seen the larger wave wash away his houses and his lands; he had noticed his brother's fright and distress. He reached down the cliff, caught hold of the hand of the younger brother, and pulled him up to safety. Then with his arm about him, they faced away from the tide and the sea, and walked together toward the open door of the brightly lighted home of their father.

"And so we play [said the preacher] upon the sands of Time, building our cities, our houses and lands. So intent do we become that we do not notice that the evening draws near, that the clouds are filling the sky, that the wind is growing chill, that the tide of death is coming in, until suddenly it races over us, sweeping away from us all our earthly possessions. Often we are terrified, alone and afraid.

"But above is our Elder Brother. He has seen it all, as once he experienced it. He reaches down his hand, catches hold of our hand, and lifts us up. Putting his arm about us, we turn from this bourne of Time and Place toward a Home, brightly lighted, and with open door. Leaving the sound and foam of the sands of Time we go with him into the home of our Father, for refreshment and rest."

So far as I, one of the congregation, was concerned, his message found its mark—primarily, if not alone, by that one picture.

Again and again some member of the congregation will remember the illustrations and then later, perhaps weeks later, from those illustrations be able to put together again the thought and argument of your sermon. On some dark morning he will be able to lift the shade and see the light of helpful thought come streaming in through the window of your illustration to give him new vision and new hope.

THE LITTLE TYKES

"The eccentric old carpenter came slowly back from the rebuilding job and paused where I was pulling up frost-killed vines in the garden," said Anne Monroe. "There was militancy in his old eyes, deep set among their wrinkles. I

20

wondered. He had gone past so cheerfully an hour earlier with his tools, all ready for work.

" 'Wouldn't let me put in any windows low, so the kiddies could see out,' he explained disgustedly. 'I said years ago, first time ever I noticed a little feller strainin' up on his toes, pullin' till his little fingertips was red, tryin' to see out, I'd never build another house without windows in it just for the likes of him. And I've kept my word. In my houses,' he added stubbornly, 'kiddies has got to have a chance to see out!'

"He glanced up with weather-wise old eyes. 'Goin' to snow,' he threw in. Then rambled on: 'Ever notice a little tyke, when the first snowflakes come, strainin' his little self up, tryin' to see? Maybe there's snowbirds hoppin' round, or a squirrel runnin' up a tree, but he can't see nuthin'! Get that sight once, and you won't build no more houses without windows in 'em somewheres for him.' " [3]

If the philosophy of the carpenter becomes that of the preacher, children will not need to strain to see in and out of his sermons. They will delight to be in his congregation.

SYMBOLISM OFTEN THE KEY

It is also to our advantage in this connection that religion lends itself to imagery, to drama, to graphic picturization.

On this Christmas morning I look out the window of my study across the glistening snow-covered streets and lawns to the homes beyond. Even now at mid-morning, with the sun shining brightly, there are the lighted Christmas trees around which but a few hours ago the bright-eyed children danced gleefully as they received their Christmas gifts. My thinking carries me back across the days of the immediate past. Taken from its most pagan to its most Christian extremes, this season finds its reality in symbols and pictures.

Whether it be the carols sung in cathedral, country chapel, or over the radio; whether it be the gifts sold entirely for profit or bought to gladden a child's heart; whether it be another act of kindness rendered by some person filled with Christ-love or the coin a hardened business man tosses into the Salvation Army kettle; whether it be the sudden repentance of a man who forgives his neighbor because of recalled childhood associations, or the upsurging of human hearts in an almost universal longing for surcease from war: however multitudinous be these feelings and expressions which surround Christmas, invariably they center in a scene, a picture, or many of them associated with the Nativity: shepherds, a star, wise men, an angelic chorus, the holy family, a Babe wrapped in swaddling clothes and lying in a manger.

What would Christmas be without the traditional scenes of the Nativity? Certainly something far less than it is. These scenes are not rationalized logic, but they are symbolism and picturesqueness. In large measure it is in the simplicity, beauty, and drama of the event which people visualize that the fascination of Christmas and its enduring power lies. In every phase of our religion the interpretations are best revealed through symbol, illustration, pictures. All religion is associated with life, drama, events, the touch of the Divine upon the life of man through the ages.

With such power in picturization, why should we preachers neglect so great an aid, why use so seldom the drama of life which will create and recreate spiritual values among our people?

Religion has always been presented by prophets and seers so that people might visualize, feel, and be moved to action. It has always been so; with Isaiah, with Jesus, and with the great preachers of the ages since. Preaching is the telling of stories, the events of living Biblical characters like David and Paul, the revelation of God to men like Amos, John Knox, and the humblest present-day mother, the leading of a nation by God; and it is supremely the story of One Man, Jesus.

THE NEW RESPONSIBILITY

Many others, novelists, editors, song writers, artists, cynics, materialists, are drawing pictures of contemporary life. A torrential flood of imagery pours from the press and the platform. Much of it is obscene, false, or pernicious. With what bright and glowing colors some paint the allurements of the world, and with what dark and earthy grotesqueness others commit humanity to the pit. Many of these representations are like the futurist painting reported to have won first prize at an art exhibit. After the award had been made it was discovered that the painting had been upside down. It is the terrifying responsibility of the preacher of today to draw a representation of life that is true, that is

Christlike, when all the old standards of art are gone and the new ones used by cynic and materialist are as untrue and absurd whether right side up or upside down.

A new responsibility has come to the preacher. It is like the new obligations upon the President of the United States. In the history of this American nation the President has been expected to supervise and lead in political matters, in governmental affairs, in the welfare of national institutions. But now for the first time in the experiences of our country the American people hold the President responsible not only for the proper functioning of government but also for the entire public existence, for economic security, for crime prevention, for prosperity or depression, for social conditions such as unemployment and poverty in old age.

In like manner the place of the preacher has changed. During the Christian centuries the preacher dealt with the ruling concepts of the Bible, of doctrine, and of the Church. In the last two generations preachers are called upon to reckon with ruling ideas prevailing in the world more than with traditional conceptions prevailing in the Church. The whole political, social, and economic outlook of modern man has demanded of the preacher that he take into account a kaleidoscopically changing world. For the first time Christianity is permitted to enter, must enter if it is to gain any directive place in the future, into social as well as new individual affairs never before opened to it. Christianity must penetrate situations paganized through the ages, fortified and buttressed by accepted customs, armed with a desperate and

24

diabolic determination to remain evil, must cleanse and spiritualize this whole current of modern life, or else fail this generation and the future as well.

For such an undertaking new approaches are needed, new methods must be devised, old ideals cloaked in modern terms. There must be furnished new words, modern understandings, novel pictures, and a renewed vision of the Eternal in the midst of Time. Phrases, terms, theological outlooks, examples, and illustrations must be reconstructed to fit a new day and a new world.

The Idlewild Presbyterian Church in Memphis is modern and up-to-date in all equipment and appointments. Its plant is entirely modern, yet it is constructed in an ecclesiastical tradition of the time when glass windows were first made. To carry out the architectural scheme, glass for the windows was constructed as it had been in those early days, with flaws, air bubbles, faint colorings, and casual imperfections. Fitting into this church as they do, these old windows become a thing of beauty and a joyous blending into a harmonious effect.

Yet what a far step from these early, imperfect, odd-shaped pieces of glass to the windows of the modern world. Today they are perfectly clear, tensile in strength, shaped and sized from the double strength of the home to the plate glass of the shop, from the translucent panes of privacy to the factories lined with rows of clear transparency, and on to the shatter-proof or bullet-proof windows of motor cars and teller's cages. So likewise is the preacher compelled to change his figures of speech, his illuminations, his parables from those suited to a bygone day to those fitting the pressing and ever-changing conceptions of the modern world.

It was so with Hosea and Isaiah, with Paul, and essentially so with the Master. The preachers of the Christian centuries also have suited their messages and figures of speech to their own times. Particularly does the same necessity rest upon the preachers of this generation. While Eternal Truth, the fundamental verities, may be the same, the essential needs of man still the same, yet they must be interpreted in terms of the contemporary.

Not by Sound Doctrine Alone

This fresh interpretation cannot be in terms of theology or ideas or doctrine alone. It will need to be picturesque, flashed out in a blaze of illumination. Truth is made known by object lessons. Parables are more ancient than arguments and far more lasting. When we preach to children we use stories, but when we preach to children grown large we hesitate to do so. Our purpose as preachers is to describe the indescribable; to illumine artfully that which can be enlightened only by imaginative insight; to portray the Divine and spiritual in terms of the temporal; to make comprehensible through imagination that which is of the realm of the spirit, the more-than-human. It is through the art of illustration, a part of the greater art of preaching, more than through any other means that people are brought to see, to feel, to act. It is more than mental persuasion which is needed. It is both understanding and commitment to a cause, the emotional set of character which produces Christlike action. There is no substitute for thinking—there is little enough of that—but normally what men need most is the impelling conviction to practice at all costs what they already know to be true.

WINDOWS ARE NOT HOUSES

I am fully aware that windows are not houses, that there is a substantial building with foundation and superstructure of truth and argument; but I am also aware that for most of us houses would be dull affairs indeed without windows. Let us warn ourselves that illustrations are not substitutes for thought and that, while they may have argumentative force of their own, they are but assistants to clear thinking. A sermon is something more than stories. Every worth-while message must be a revelation of solid truth.

If one had to choose between the solid structure of reason and intellectual insight and the windows of illustration, certainly one would choose the former. If we confine our study to the windows, it is not because we have forgotten the rest of the building. It is because we realize that while we as preachers may enjoy discussing abstract truth, our congregations are made up of people who must readily eye the truth we preach.

John Wesley's advice to his preachers was full of sound sense as he quoted from the words of Aristotle, "Though you think with the learned, you must speak with the common people." And the people live in the world of pictures. Whatever your theological or social or Biblical outlook,

27

make people see. Convince them by having them visualize the truth you preach.

Artists of the Eternal

Sermon illustration is one of the fine arts, but it is not preaching. Indeed, as Bishop Quayle has said, "Preaching is not the art of making a sermon and delivering it. Preaching is the art of making a preacher and delivering that." It is true that every work of art is a revelation of its composer, sculptor, painter, preacher. However great the art or the artist there has been a time, long or short, of acquiring the skill, in which the genius ripened to maturity. For instance, everyone skilled with the brush must have been taught or have learned for himself the technique of mixing and blending colors. While every painter has hundreds of color shades from which to choose, some colors fade with time, others absorb near-by colors, some endure. It is no small part of art to be able to choose the exact color shade and to use it with skill.

Rembrandt's high position among the most eminent painters is in large measure due to his treatment of light and shade, and to his subtle use of color. Yet he never uses light for its own sake, but always as an instrument of projection and as an expression of the invisible and imponderable.

Likewise painters of eternal truth enrich the divine message by skillfully using the lights and shades of human experience and the subtle as well as bold colors of imagination.

Preachers are artists of the eternal, and a vital part of that artistry is illustration. It is given to men to be preachers, and God calls those who are to paint his glories. Preaching is an art, a gift, and yet it can be developed. As Rembrandt spent his whole early life experimenting, testing, and learning, so preachers may well devote themselves to mastering the elements of their artistry that in the fullness of time they too may produce the sermonic masterpieces.

II

THE MASTER STORYTELLER

HISTORY should pay tribute to certain unknown heroes among the most primitive men of our race. Along with the names of the foremost inventors and discoverers should be placed, if we only knew it, the name of the one who first learned the use of fire, and that of the man who first learned how to use a wheel (the American Indians never discovered it, always dragging their burdens on long poles as runners). These men made great contributions to human progress.

To these should be added the name of the person who told the first story or recited the first tale and began an art which is older than painting, sculpturing, literature, and probably as old as music. Perhaps it was Mrs. Eve or Mrs. Stonehatchet as she gathered her children close to her and gave them the first bedtime story, or possibly Mr. Adam or Mr. Stonehatchet, when before a campfire he graphically recited his achievements in the hunt or described the terror that stalked beyond the firelight.

Storytelling is as ancient as language and as modern as this moment! At this very instant countless multitudes of persons are reciting incidents and events, or describing imaginative scenes. Mothers, teachers in schoolrooms, children at play, people on the streets or in social gatherings, orators in courtrooms or statehouses, preachers in churches or in private homes are telling stories for enjoyment or persuasion.

It has been an honorable art, even though perverted on occasions. Throughout the ages it has found a central place in religion, preachers and prophets using incidents and illustrations that they might make clear the relationship of the spiritual to the life of man. Taking this method of communication of ideas and ideals they have lifted it to the highest place of usefulness.

In Biblical days those who wished to proclaim their divine message often found it could best be done by relating an incident which would stimulate the imagination. Isaiah visions his call in the temple and again pictures the Suffering Servant; Hosea compares a broken home with a broken-hearted God; Amos indicts his age with the skillful recital of nations wrecked by their godlessness, and measures his own people by the plumbline. Daniel and the faithful are used to encourage a people harassed and persecuted by those who would destroy the faith.

There is no Old Testament picture more packed with significance than Isaiah 53: "He was despised, and rejected of men; a man of sorrows, and acquainted with grief: and we hid as it were our faces from him; he was despised, and we esteemed him not. Surely he hath borne our griefs, and car-

31

ried our sorrows: yet we did esteem him stricken, smitten of God, and afflicted. But he was wounded for our transgressions, he was bruised for our iniquities: the chastisement of our peace was upon him; and with his stripes we are healed. All we like sheep have gone astray; we have turned every one to his own way; and the Lord hath laid on him the iniquity of us all."

Preachers of the Christian Centuries

In like manner the preachers of the Christian centuries have been using this method of illuminating truth. The best preachers have been masters of illustration, every century producing fine examples. A study of the history of preaching from this viewpoint yields valuable reinforcement to our use of the same method.

Certain preachers in the centuries past are described by Dr. A. E. Garvie in the *Christian Preacher*. Frail Richard Baxter was given by Nature no advantage "except a glowing eye and a moving voice." His was serious preaching "as a dying man to dying men." He felt keenly, and envisioned the Kingdom so that all might see.[1]

Jeremy Taylor, whose *Holy Living* and *Holy Dying* are still regarded as religious classics, is described as "a brilliant author-preacher, who is as prodigal with his wealth of anecdote 'as an Asiatic queen with her pearls.' "[2]

Charles Haddon Spurgeon of the nineteenth century still casts his shadow over the twentieth. "It was not mere theology he preached; his truth was often embodied in a tale, and the arrow of his appeal was winged with a wise and witty saying. His wide and keen observation of life, his varied reading, supplied him with abundant illustrations of the doctrine he set forth. His preaching was natural, without pulpit affectation; he talked with fullness and freshness of thought. He knew how to make even an ordinary subject interesting by unhackneyed exposition and illustration." [3]

During the same time Thomas Guthrie, the Scotch prince of illustrators, "knew how to reach the hearts of the common people, and was the master of what may be called pictorial preaching. Few preachers have so aimed at presenting truth in a tale. 'An illustration,' he says, 'or an example drawn from nature, a Bible story or any history will, like a nail, often hang up a thing which otherwise would fall to the ground. . . . Mind the three P's. In every discourse the preacher should aim at PROVING, PAINTING, and PERSUADING; in other words, addressing the Reason, the Fancy, and the Heart.'" [4]

Frederick W. Robertson's sensitive and powerful sermons had an irresistible appeal. "They are based on a constant and minute study of the Scriptures; they breathe the spirit of intense devoutness; they are most searching in their scrutiny of the experience and character of men; they are illumined by illustrations drawn from varied and accurate study; . . . and the center is in Christ the Saviour." [5]

Henry Ward Beecher was a man of vivid imagination and intense passion, extraordinarily dramatic. "He was constantly studying his Bible, the world around him, the men he met, reading, observing, meditating with one object, to gather material for his pulpit." [6]

The pre-eminent preacher of the last century, and possibly of the American pulpit, was Phillips Brooks. He gave untiring labor to sermon preparation. "He was a very hard worker, a very diligent student, reading widely 'science, literature, biography, history, poetry;' but the one thing he did was to preach, using all else for this end." [7]

These are but a few of those who during the years both before and after the advent of Christ have used this method of illustration which so easily wins its way into the hearts, wills, and deeds of the people.

WHO CAN VIE WITH JESUS?

Everywhere there have been those who sought through verbal picturing, real and imagined, to entertain or influence people. But what teller of stories, East or West, ancient or modern, can compare with Jesus?

Best sellers among novels and short stories may run a hundred thousand or so, perhaps more, but the stories of Jesus have sold by hundreds of millions and have been read or heard by literally billions of people. They have been read and reread again and again until they have become fixed in the memory of multitudes. Jesus is the unrivaled Teller of Stories.

The marvel of these stories of Jesus is that in every age they prove their startling modernity. Told nineteen hundred years ago, they are as recent as today's newspaper. Parables were recounted long before Jesus, and incidents have been told this very morning, yet his continue to be the most memorable and the most popular. Their message is as timeless as God Himself.

We may compare unfavorably the simple times in which Jesus lived with our modern, complex, highly organized social order, and yet the parable of the prodigal son rings true in all ages. "When our clever sciences have been forgotten, when all other stories pall, when the earth waxes old like a garment, this story will still be young. It will still have power to untangle our raveled life. It will still win us to our hearts' true home." [8]

Vast Range of the Parables

In the crowds who listened to Jesus were all peoples, children and aged, the strong and the weak, the poverty-stricken and the wealthy, stalwart youth and decrepit age, men and women, saints and sinners. They were a cross section of humanity.

His stories reveal the fact that his observation was as wide as life and as deep as God. There were the king, his courtiers and his follies; wars, feasts, and treaties; the judge solemnly pronouncing doom upon prisoners; the proprietor and his servants of different temperaments and ethical judgments; the merchant, well prepared, going on the long journey, and hoping for adventurous wealth; and the banker and the pearl merchant.

The simple life abounded in similarities to him: fishermen,

shepherds, agriculturists, laborers unemployed, the father and his two sons of such different and vulnerable dispositions, the ambushed traveler, encountered by a busy priest, a prominent churchman and a foreigner, and the celebration of the wedding feast with bride, groom, and attendants.

Although the stories of Jesus are not many, through them we learn of his times, the most intimate aspects of his land, and the very life of his age. We see the deprivations of the poor, the accumulations of the rich, a woman sitting in the dim light patching an old garment, and the eager expectancy of a tenant farmer whose plow suddenly turns over a long buried treasure. About the streets the petulant children play, while their elders make mockery of religion and life's serious responsibilities. There are the socially ambitious who seek the prominent places at public gatherings.

Life is everywhere: the poor man who is rich in things alone; the charity of the underprivileged Samaritan; the hungry eyes of the unemployed whose needs are as great as those who are working; king and pauper, wealth and pennies and a barren fig tree in the midst of a barren nation. There is a woman frenzied at the loss of her wedding coin, and overjoyed at finding it. At midnight we see the emergency of the friend borrowing bread for guests unexpectedly arrived. On the journey to a strange place we behold a merchant's eyes popping out at the sight of the great pearl. "We come to a bend in the road where a prodigal boy caught sight of home." The whole gamut of human life and its varying and tempestuous emotions is engraved in unforgettable stories. With what keen eyes and preceptive insight Jesus has observed everything about him and wrought them into the warp and woof of his message.

JESUS' SERMONS ILLUSTRATED

Jesus wrote nothing, so far as we know. He certainly did not compose written sermons, nor read them. Only infrequently is it indicated that his messages were formal or for an occasion. There is, of course, the instance of the Sermon on the Mount. We are not concerned here with the critical question as to whether all in Matthew 5 to 7 was contained in one sermon delivered on a particular day, on a certain mountainside, or whether, like Luke gathering the parables together, the writer of Matthew compiled the various sermonic materials of Jesus for one event. However that may be, the conclusion to this Sermon on the Mount is apparently the final climax to the preaching of Jesus: "Act on your good intentions." The conclusion illustrates the necessity for action: success in the Christian life comes not by repeating, "Lord, Lord!" but "by entering in at the narrow gate," and "by their fruits." If you merely hear and do nothing, you are like a house on melting sands. If you hear and do, you are like a house on a foundation of solid rock.

ON THE SPUR OF THE MOMENT?

In almost every instance, however, Jesus preaches, not conventional sermons, but out of the chance remark or question of his hearers comes a spark which suddenly explodes an effective parable. Are we, as preachers, to take this as an indication that we should not attempt to prepare our sermons in advance, "for it shall be given you in that hour what ye shall speak"? [9] Quite the contrary! It is apparent from the perfect form and art of every one of the parables that they came from a full life, careful and penetrating thought, and have the marks of preparation. Those questions and remarks of his contemporaries, which seemed impetuous and immediate, were to Jesus matters that he had considered thoughtfully and deeply all during his life.

He had seen a shepherd who had lost a sheep. An impression was fixed forever, undoubtedly connected with the shepherd's psalm. Again, how often he had seen a prodigal son, knew a brokenhearted father, perhaps Joseph as one of the younger brothers in his own family had been wayward. The intimate contact with man and with his Heavenly Father brought into focus again and again the incidents of life as they related to the two. When those about him raised questions, Jesus from an abundant and thoughtful life gave the answers, not so much ready-made as fully seasoned. To be effective followers of Jesus we must continually search for the proper and fitting to illustrate the truth of his Kingdom.

THE LITERARY FORM

Many of the most arrowlike illustrations of Jesus, which forever remain barbed in the memory, are brief metaphors and similes—"Ye are the salt of the earth, the light of the world; a city set on a hill cannot be hid; enter in by the narrow gate; the lamp of the body is the eye." There is a stark and startling reality to many of his pictures: "If thine eye cause thee to stumble, pluck it out, and cast it from thee." [10]

His parables are the short-story art at its finest. Without the waste of a word, his consummate skill leads through the scene and character immediately to the climax. There is no irrelavance, no diversion, no inadvertence. The unessential is omitted. And yet no one can imagine an improvement upon the form of the stories. They include the moral question considered in its entirety. The aptitude and fitness of each of his stories is without doubt beyond criticism. He has chosen the exact situation to suit the occasion and put it into words that remain forever engraved on the memory. The form of his illustrations deserves much time and study from those who would likewise teach the truth of their Master.

Plagiarism

Something will be said later of plagiarism. It never bothered Jesus any more than it did Shakespeare. It seems quite evident that the Old Testament parable of the vineyard in Isaiah 5: 1-7 was rebuilt by Jesus with new vision and telling force.[11] Jesus did not say, "I have read a parable by the 'first' Isaiah which carries a fine point, but which I have enlarged and present to you in a form more suited to our day," and then proceed with the parable of the vineyard. He simply drew the finer picture, without cumbersome explanations. Perhaps in this he can exorcise some demons which plague sensitive souls.

Often Jesus acknowledges, as preachers must, where the source definitely needs to be recognized or where it adds reinforcement to the message: "Jesus saith unto them, Did ye never read in the *scriptures,*

> The stone which the builders rejected,
> The same was made the head of the corner;
> This was from the Lord,
> And it is marvelous in our eyes?" [12]

Each a Gem

The parables are not organized by Jesus into a logical or synthetic unity. He made no attempt to work out a complete system. They were not given as systematic teaching nor grouped like gems in a jewelry store, all of a particular kind gathered to themselves. Among the parables here is a ruby, there a diamond, again an amethyst, each with an exquisite beauty all its own. Each story by itself is a jewel with beauty, grace, and power,

> "Fair as a star, when only one
> Is shining in the sky." [13]

The New Land

If Columbus were to return to America after four hundred and fifty years, what a change he would find! He would discover truly a new world. How would he compare his little boats with the Leviathan and Queen Mary, an Indian village with New York City, his arrows and muzzleloading rifles with modern siege guns? What would he think of the automobile, electric lights, radio, and the airship circling the entire earth in a few days? He would find what we say he discovered—a *new* world.

With Jesus through his stories we enter into an amazing new world of wonderment and surprise, the Land of Spiritual Realities, as far above our world as our age is beyond that of Columbus. It is the land of Utopia, the land of the Ideal, the Kingdom of God. But it is not a mythical, unrealizable goal. It is the country some people reach on this earth today and at which all the world shall arrive on some fair To-morrow.

To Jesus all Nature and human life were parables to reveal the unseen life of God. He had no other purpose in telling these remarkable insights. Jesus saw a divine likeness between the Kingdom of God, which we think of as heaven, and the Kingdom of God as a practical reality upon earth. " 'Heaven' to us may be a dream of earth, but to him earth was a broken and shadowy reflection of heaven." [14]

Edwin Markham has a poem which well might be thought of as an interpretation of Jesus' vision through the parables:

> "We men of earth have here the stuff
> Of paradise—we have enough!
> We need no other stones to build
> The stairs into the Unfulfilled—
> No other ivory for the doors—
> No other marble for the floors—

41

> No other cedar for the beam
> And dome of man's immortal dream.
>
> Here on the paths of every day—
> Here on the common human way—
> Is all the busy gods would take
> To build a Heaven, to mold and make
> New Edens. Ours the task sublime
> To build eternity in time." [15]

SIGNPOSTS

We are like weary travelers in a strange country, lost in the forests in a wild storm at night. Our greatest danger is that we wander in circles or go crashing blindly into the pitfalls. Intermittently through the wind and driving rain, brilliant lightning flashes show the landmarks and we manage to keep our course.

The parables are not dreary details of the road, but lightning flashes from God in the night, brilliantly revealing the high promontories and landmarks of life, and by them we can manage to find our way.

Jesus presented truth as no man before or since, but he realized that logic is not life, that the spiritual cannot be proved by argumentation. In its finality truth is not a theology, a metaphysic, or even factual science. It is Spirit and the light of life.

The parables without the life of Jesus could not stand alone, and yet one who knows the stories understands the teachings and the heart of the great Teacher. We need merely to read or hear these matchless masterpieces of literary style and human understanding "to realize how swiftly they arouse the imagination, smite the conscience, and quicken the will." [16]   These stories in themselves have power to transform and change life. How many a person has heard the story of the Good Shepherd and felt anew the warming love of God! How many a person has thought of the friend seeking bread at midnight and in the dark necessity of his own soul gone imploring God for the bread of life! How many a wayward human being has through the story of the prodigal son turned to the forgiving love of the Father God!

Jesus saw and we, his minister-followers, need to recognize that in the working of the human mind and the Providence of God, the Spirit can find its way into human action through illustrations as through no other means. Somehow the Word slips through the minister's word pictures and becomes in human flesh a living reality.

THE DAILY WAY

A large number of the parables are concerned with personal conduct, daily tasks, inward spiritual discernment, attitudes toward others, the relationship between man and God. There are the similitudes—the Kingdom is like the mustard seed, the leaven, a pearl of great price. . . . There is the perplexing question, always perplexing, of the presence of evil like tares. Responsibilities, duties, privileges, earnestness are portrayed. There are injunctions to humility, forgiveness, true neighborliness, and warnings about the use of wealth, lest a soul feed on the husks of things. The forgiveness and love of God are beautifully and appealingly pictured—a God of the lost.

As we ministers face the same necessities of the daily life of our people, we, following the Master, will attempt so to envision and picture the events and occurrences of every day that the people may live worthily and nobly, realizing the continuing presence of their daily Companion, the Christlike God.

THE CRISIS

Some of the parables had to do, not with matters of normal behavior, but with sudden opposition, grave crisis. Jesus recognized that there were two ways of facing a crisis where the odds were overwhelmingly against one. The first was by rushing into the fray, precipitating the issue, and taking the consequences, silenced either by prison or death. The other method was by skillfully avoiding an open break, not by side-stepping but by facing the issue more realistically through indirection.

If one craves the notoriety of the martyr, the first thing to do is to join issue with the overpowering forces of evil and be gloriously vanquished. Many are the martyrs who have advanced the Kingdom—and who could have done so in no other manner. Yet if one has the far more important mission of revealing God and the truth, he may need to choose the other weapon of parable. In so doing he may not always save the present situation, but he will at least instill the undying hope in the Remnant.

Jesus followed this latter course—not of
he willingly chose the cross when the time cam
the one who was "wise as a serpent but harmless
Had he in the first few months contended with the
his truth would have been immediately snuffed ou
better it was to teach those who would be faithful and ...ve
the others bewildered. Only one way was possible in this
emergency—that of parable and story.

With what insight into both human nature and the critical
social situation he tells why he uses parabolic teaching—that
those who have eyes to see may perceive and the unbelievers
may neither see nor understand. On one occasion he quotes
from Isaiah, changing the wording slightly, but the meaning
greatly. Isaiah had stated that the responsibility for the
unseeing eyes and unhearing ears of his generation was God's.
Jesus places the responsibility upon the people themselves:

> "This people's heart is waxed gross,
> And their ears are dull of hearing,
> And their eyes *they* have closed." [17]

This deliberate blindness could not be overcome: exception
to their way they would immediately and violently oppose.
The majority never did understand where Jesus was going
until near the close of the Gospel story: "When the chief
priests and the Pharisees heard his parable, they perceived
that he spake of them." [18]

The sightless ones began to suspect something wrong and
attempted again and again to catch him in open statement.

When they tried to trap him with a coin, they felt sure that he would commit himself to his ruin. If he answered, "Yes, pay tribute to Caesar," he would lose prestige with the people; his influence would flee. If he answered, "No, do not pay taxes," they would eagerly have cause to put him into prison. But instead he left an enduring picture that condemned the religious pietists and political zealots of his day and every day, and also an ideal of devotion unto God that shall never be forgotten: "Render unto Caesar—and unto God."

Unto the end he tried to win those who might yet at this late hour open their eyes to reality. The parable with a few might be a seed, sown in untilled soil, yet perchance springing to life and yielding fruit. It did so with Nicodemus and Joseph of Arimathea. Instance also the parable of the two sons.[19]

Even his approach to Jerusalem was a parable enacted. To have proclaimed publicly his messiahship would have brought immediate imprisonment. So he rode into Jerusalem on an ass. To the wise and sophisticated it was just another pilgrim come to the feast. But to those who remembered the prophecy, it was the humble approach of the Deliverer, the new King. Those who were puzzled, raised critical questions, while those of vision cried, "Hosanna, the Son of David, coming in the name of the Lord." He made no verbal claim, so the chiefs stood sullenly by, impotent!

This method of Jesus had been used before, but never with the fruitfulness with which he portrayed for all the ages the realities of the Kingdom. During the Syrian deluge of destruction upon the Jewish people prior to the Christian era, the stories contained in the book of Daniel were widely circulated. In the very presence of the Syrian guard, they were read, for they seemed but foolish tales. Yet to the harassed and faithful Jews it was the light of hope and courage and fidelity even while they were surrounded by lions or going through the fiery furnace.

This method has been used often since Jesus. Henry Ward Beecher relates that upon his first Sunday at his first appointment he was met by the board of elders, who told him they wanted him to preach upon any themes of the Gospel he chose, but that upon the first occasion of his mentioning "abolition," they would immediately vote him out of his pulpit.

He contemplated his position. He could go into the pulpit that morning, deliver himself upon his conviction, bravely. Of course that would be his last sermon to that congregation. He did preach that morning and every Sunday for several years. He later related, "During those years I never mentioned the words 'abolition' or 'slavery,' but I preached continuously and repeatedly upon those themes by indirection until I believe that when I was ready to leave that pulpit for another more than half of the congregation were definitely opposed to human slavery."

Dr. George Buttrick tells how an epidemic of card-playing swept through his congregation, more contagious than the measles. He knew that this was not a mortal sin and that there were evils and practices far more injurious than this among his constituents. Yet it had become so serious that it was paralyzing the women's activities of the church and community. He knew he could not preach a sermon on card-playing. A frontal attack would be merely laughed away. Yet something had to be done. For more than a month he worried as to how to proceed so as to do more than condemn a practice.

Finally it was solved by a little girl who unwittingly gave him his sermon. One afternoon her mother put her to bed, explaining that she was again entertaining the bridge club. She said, "Darling, you rest this afternoon and when you are finished with your nap, play here in the nursery until mother comes up for you. Mother has the ladies over this afternoon."

Considerable time passed; the child awakened and played about the nursery, but soon becoming lonesome, she ventured out into the hall. Down the wide winding stairs the little figure came, still dressed in her pajamas. When she was about halfway down, she saw her mother on the far side of one of the rooms and called loudly, "Mother!"

The interruption had come at the most inopportune moment. There had been a chill silence over the tables as the women had watched their cards closely. In the next few moments the decision would be made as to who won the coveted prize. Angrily the women turned to see where the disturbance came from. From the spacious rooms all could see the little pajama-clad child, and she called again, "Mother, don't any of these women have homes?"

Dr. Buttrick says that the story of the little girl convinced these wise women that they did have homes, husbands, and children, and a church which they had been sadly neglecting for trivial and unimportant playthings. This story could do more than any number of sermons on "card-playing."

OUR PROCEDURE

Stories and parables and illustrations like our Master's will bring home the life of the spirit to our people. On any Sunday and under any circumstance it will prove the most effective way of leaving the indelible impression. In the sermons on joy, meekness, forgiveness, temperance it will have prominent place.

This method of Jesus is most significant to us as we face the present world crisis, which undoubtedly will grow more and more critical. Shall we make the issue final now between the Way and the evil forces of lawlessness, political intrigue, religious institutionalism, fiendish multimillioned murder— and be ostracized, go to prison or death? There will come many instances where we will need to encounter the enemy, face to face and hand to hand, boldly stating the truth, regardless of the consequences.

But our purpose is not martyrdom. It is to convert the world and to win the people, the Remnant at least, to Jesus' way of life. It may be wisest rather to paint and picture the issues in colors that any who have eyes may see, or ears may hear, and thus for themselves choose the way of life. Shall we not, like John in the Revelation, convict our age with pictures of Beasts and Fiends, and at the same time bring comfort to our besieged friends with scenes of a City, Holy, above the chaos of earth, whose Builder and Maker is God?

No minister of Jesus Christ, "who for the joy that was set before him endured the cross," can afford to dodge the issues, turn his back upon the right, or fail to indict evil. But he must choose his method—if he uses that of story and illustration, it will be alone because Jesus and his Way shall be glorified.

Perhaps the difficulties may not be so acute for some ministers, even, perchance, for all of us. Yet the method of the Master Storyteller will prove useful to us in the everyday responsibilities of the parish church. No minister of Jesus Christ will depreciate the use of illustration and story in the sermon. Rather, following his Master, he will attempt to make the greatest and most sacred use of all illustrative material that the Kingdom might more readily come.

III

VARIETIES OF ILLUSTRATIONS AND THEIR USE

IN the builders trade is found an unbelievably large number of window patterns, and new ones are being designed continually. For every type of house there are specifically devised casements. For bank, church, home, school, or factory there are different makes, and for each of these there are innumerable varieties from which to select.

Church windows may be oblong openings in a white-walled meetinghouse, arched windows of a Romanesque design, or the art glass monuments of a great cathedral. Their materials may be the hideous sepulchral blue, yellow, and purple panes found in certain small churches, frosted glass letting in the softened light, or delicately shaded characters wrought by Tiffany's exquisite art.

There are as varied and infinite possibilities in the windows which may illumine sermons as there are in the builder's trade. What a pity that with such a vast store of materials any congregation is forced to live in the darkness of un-illuminated thought!

In this chapter we shall enter the show room of the Sermonic Sash and Door Company to see the vast variety of windows with their fascinating and useful designs. Here is opened to us a display which will provide a casement for every sermonic house and through which people may receive light in the gospel dwelling.

THE MAGIC OF WORDS

Illustrations may be pictures flashed out in a single word, a short combination of graphic words, or a scene described at length. All preaching must be done through symbols we know as words.

> "Words are
> The silver notes
> That ring the chord of sound
> And play the colored symphony
> Of speech." [1]

"The Word" is the majestic title of the Son of God. The awful responsibility upon one who would feel free to expound the Word of God is contained often in the Scriptures, particularly in these two accounts recorded in Matthew:

"And whosoever speaketh a word against the Son of man, it shall be forgiven him: but whosoever speaketh against the Holy Ghost, it shall not be forgiven him, neither in this world, neither in the world to come." [2]

"And I say unto you, that every idle word that men shall speak, they shall give account thereof in the day of judgment.

For by thy words thou shalt be justified, and by thy words thou shalt be condemned." [3]

Words are the material out of which the preacher creates the living body of his sermon. By their improper use his sermon halts and limps, too frail to carry the burdens of the congregation. Or by enlightened thought his message may take wings and his people be lifted into the celestial realm and fed on manna divine.

ONE WORD

Let us begin this study with the simplest form of verbal picturization—a single word. Often an illumination may be in just one word. A picture unforgettable may be expressed in a familiar word placed in an unusual order in the sentence. The verb is more descriptive than the adjective. Each word in language has a meaning shaded to a certain usage and to none other. Choosing the familiar and exact one makes a sermon easily understood, giving it the power of conviction.

Consider the use of language by Jesus. Where have words ever been used with more clarity or force? Start any place among any of his parables and begin to dissect. Study, for instance, the words in this parable of the lost sheep: "And he spake unto them this parable, saying, What man of you, having a hundred sheep, and having lost one of them, doth not leave the ninety and nine in the wilderness, and go after that which is lost, until he find it? And when he hath found it, he layeth it on his shoulders, rejoicing. And when he cometh home, he calleth together his friends and his neighbors, saying unto them, Rejoice with me, for I have found my sheep which was lost. I say unto you, that even so there shall be joy in heaven over one sinner that repenteth, more than over ninety and nine righteous persons, who need no repentance." [4]

Leave out any word you please and the picture is marred and disfigured. Put in any word and you have not added one iota to the description, the scene, or the value of the truth. For instance, leave out the word "rejoicing." The entire story is marred; for it is in this word that the atmosphere of the story is created. Upon the joy of the shepherd depends the rejoicing of the neighbors and the heavenly host. Yet to describe at length what was meant by this feeling would weaken rather than strengthen the connotation.

This parable has been paraphrased countless times, but has never been improved upon. The graphic method used by Jesus so impressed those who heard him that when the time came, years later, for his words to be recorded, it was a comparatively easy undertaking.

Words carry their own character; some ring true, others are counterfeit, and perhaps more than any phase of a minister's life his speech betrayeth or commendeth him. Out of the heart the mouth speaketh, and the man is revealed according to his thoughts expressed in speech.

Diction is a primary consideration for the preacher. We preach to a modern age and our language needs to be contemporary. There is a place for scientific terms in sermons today, but the preacher's primary need is to master words which convey images and stir thought currents.

THE POWER OF A METAPHOR

Next to single words are those pictures formed by a short combination of words, a metaphor or a simile. How often Jesus used them and with what perpetuating power! There are fifty-six metaphors in the brief Sermon on the Mount. "Ye are the salt of the earth, the light of the world. A city set on a hill cannot be hid. The lamp of the body is the eye." [5]

Here are a few modern sermonic metaphors, similes and phrases, chosen from several of the most forceful modern preachers. Notice how there is not a single word in any of them which is outside the range of the average intelligence. It is their freshness, the unusual arrangement of ordinary words, which gives them pertinence.

"As futile as an old mistake." [6] Is there anything more hopeless than wishing vainly to undo an old error or wrong? "As vague and meaningless as an embalmed deity." [7] Those who are "wistful but unconvinced." "Flowerbeds in the foreground of life can never fully take the place of mountains in its background." [8] "What do we mean—everything coming out all right? My friends, Calvary is only six miles from Bethlehem." [9] "The earth is seamed with chasms. It is bitter with grudges, red with blood, and hollow with graves." [10] These are all common words, but in unusual and impressive order.

The *Reader's Digest* carries an interesting column entitled "Towards a More Picturesque Speech." [11] Some selections from it pierce our dull consciousness: "Red-haired autumn." "The day snailed by." "The wrinkled half of my life." "The bells and clocks of the town were discussing midnight." "The dog buttoned down his tail and made a beeline for shelter."

Several pointed similes include, "abrupt as a slammed door," "irrevocable as a haircut," "as involved as spaghetti," "terse as a prescription."

Sermon Subjects

While it may be somewhat apart from our theme, it might be well to add that sermon subjects are like windows which open into a home on a dark night. The passer-by sees into the living-room. Under the illumination of a floor lamp or two the family are circled about, reading or listening to the radio. There is not enough light to throw all the activities into a focus, but just enough to suggest the comforts and attractiveness of a happy home.

The purpose of an announced sermon subject is to make attractive to prospective visitors the inviting interior. It should be captivating, alluring, interesting, and suggestive. It should illuminate the message enough so that persons would want to hear it, but it should not be so matter of fact or so flatly stated as to arouse no anticipation or interest.

This certainly is no plea for sensational topics or shocking themes. When a minister once announced the subject, "The

Best Town in the World by a Dam Site," he attracted a crowd, but he added little to the Christian Gospel. The most repulsive subject I have ever chanced upon is the following: "What Goes Over the Old Devil's Back Must Come Under His Belly."

On the other hand, a preacher who announces outworn stock-in-trade phrasing will find that he adds nothing to the Gospel's appeal and, what is more, the people will not be drawn to his services. A bulletin board on a busy street corner announced next Sunday's sermon: "Repentance—A Requirement of Salvation." In that announced subject the preacher had told it all. What young man passing down the street and throwing a hurried glance at that signboard would be interested enough to say to himself, "I must hear that"? Undoubtedly he would need the guidance it would give, but the stereotyped and uninteresting phrasing would not arrest his attention. "A Requirement of Salvation" would be better, or, better still, "Give Me Another Chance," [12] or "Thank God—and Repent." [13]

There is something for every one of us preachers to ponder in the experience of an elderly minister friend of mine in a Southern city, as he met a physician parishioner on the street one day. The doctor said, "Brother Smith, I noticed in the newspaper that you have announced to preach on the subject, 'The Good Samaritan.' Do you realize that I in my lifetime have heard a number of preachers expound that Scripture, and have, myself, taught it in the Sunday-school lessons more times than I can remember? My first reaction was to stay at home, except that I knew you would present your message in a way to do me good."

Suppose that preacher had chosen the subject for that evening which Dr. J. W. G. Ward announced when he preached on the same Scripture, "Ambushed: A Tale of a Traveler." [14] Would not the doctor and possibly others have come with expectancy rather than with the stale feeling that they were having too much of a good thing?

Make your sermon titles command attention, stir the imagination, and create a desire within the prospective attendant to hear what you have to say.

Here are a few intriguing titles: "Is Religion a Frozen Asset?" [15] "Get Out of My Way." [16] "Suburban Christians." [17] "Move On." [18] "Courage for the Unknown." [19] "The High Cost of Low Living." [20] "The Unemployed Carpenter." [21] "To the Perplexed." [22] "The Unknown Soldier Speaks." [23] "Blundering into Paradise." [24] "What's the Use of a Conscience?" [25] "What May I Expect from My Religion?" [26] "Little Evils That Lay Waste Life." [27] "The Land of Beginning Again." [28]

STUDY WORDS

With the exception of abstract words, all others are symbols and create within the hearer's mind pictures, some more vivid than others. Wise is that preacher who builds into his vocabulary those words and language combinations which are most expressive. We preach to a modern age and our language needs to be contemporary, but it also needs to have

some of that depth and insight which we in
"classic."

The vocabulary which any person has is larg
direction. Much of it is due to his environm
versation in his early home life, the language he
companions and at school, and then what he has ...oed
from reading. While this is true, it is also possible to extend
one's vocabulary widely and in the direction one desires.

The principal method is to read and read and read. Books
which are considered good literature are invaluable. A
preacher does great injustice to his own mind to read another man's sermon in order to repreach the other man's
message, but he strengthens his own preaching when he reads
another's sermons to study that man's methods. In this
connection he will note the skillful transition of thought, the
use of words, exact and clear, the power of simile, and how
the incidents are graphically told.

The terms and phrases of modern language have become
more scientific, but it certainly cannot be said that they have
become more devotional in quality. Constant reading of the
Bible will enrich a minister's thought and vocabulary as nothing else will. The greatest legal minds do it that they may
become better lawyers. How much more should those who
tread in sacred places be gripped by the power of the language of Scripture!

I asked an English professor in New York how a person
could improve his vocabulary. He said, "There is only one
way—Read! Read! Read!" It would little behoove me

There are stories, events, character delineations, humor, parables, poetry, personal experiences, dramatic scenes, flashes of illumination. All provide avenues of visualization by means of which no sermon need ever be tedious or uninspiring.

One of the most potent dangers to the minister is that his preaching may fall into a rut and, without his knowing it, Sunday after Sunday follow the same routine in outline, presentation, and materials. Studious choice of illustration, selection from different fields, the use of one type and then another of illumination will add greatly to the diversity of appeal.

The danger in variety is the sense of superficiality, its seeming failure to come to grips with life, the feeling that it is not contemporaneous reality but a frothy gloss of immaterial novelty. Yet truth is many-sided, life is drama, and if one preaches to a living generation it will be from many viewpoints and angles.

When Dr. Fred B. Fisher was at Ann Arbor he preached to one of the largest and most critical congregations in the United States. The concluding sermon of a series, "Can I Know God?" was on the subject, "The Wonder of Religious Experience." Out of the last thirteen paragraphs there are eight which begin as follows: "Luther one time said . . ., Michelangelo had one great prayer . . ., Walt Whitman cried . . ., Weird little Bernard Shaw . . ., Sam Walter Foss wrote years ago . . ., Bernard Shaw will never find . . ., Here is Albert Einstein saying . . ., J. Middleton Murry, who is a modern mystic . . ., Angela Morgan—I want to close with Angela Morgan—a beautiful soul. . . ." [29]

It sounds as you bring out those first words of each paragraph as though it were not a sermon but a hodgepodge of quotations gathered indiscriminately; and yet as you read and, I presume, more as you hear, the unity of a gloriously wonderful religious experience comes to life. Variety fills this sermon, yet it in no way depreciates the truth, rather makes it real and living. If variety is kept in harmony with fact, it should give a sense of reality and integrity. It appears that nothing is so open to differences in presentation as the message of the pulpit: all life comes within its scope.

THE STORY FEATURE

Dr. John A. Rice once said, "I wish some preacher had the nerve to walk into his pulpit some Sunday morning and without any preliminaries tell a forceful story and at the conclusion say, like Nathan, 'Thou art the man!' and then walk out."

One could hardly approve the bald setting suggested, but might well wish for a wider use of story-sermons. One such message was delivered by Dr. John Haynes Holmes, "Arms for the Fight," a powerful story-sermon indicting war. It appeared in the *Christian Century Pulpit* and was entitled, "A Children's Sermon." But why for children only? No adult could hear those graphic and dramatic situations described and be quite the same again. He might not have his inherited and acquired reactions toward war mania entirely removed by this one message, but no argumentative sermon would do more than this story to realign his emotional reactions against this world curse.

Rare, however, would be the occasion which would call forth this method of sermonizing. More to the preacher's service comes the short story which pictures an incident, fable, parable, event, scene, or personal experience as a part of the sermon. Every preacher uses these. And his effectiveness depends in no small measure upon his art in handling them. While the story feature includes other types of illustration, such as parable, event, experience, it is considered here as a separate matter because it needs an emphasis all its own. The power of these illustrations lies in the fact that they are in the form of a story.

H. A. Overstreet, in a book of practical psychological advice called *Influencing Human Behavior,* gives this admonition to public speakers: "There must be movement if we are to hold attention very long. . . . 'What is happening?' 'What is going to happen?' If one can stir either of these questions in the minds of people, students or prospective customers, or voters, etc., he has in so far captured their attention. It is for this reason that a story almost invariably holds us. The story obviously moves. Something is happening; and we wish to know the outcome. Nor is the story just a rambling movement—unless it is a poor story. It is movement TOWARDS. It carries us along—TO SOMETHING." [30]

Tell a story to your congregation and immediately the interest picks up. A sustained argument may tax their thinking powers; they perceive the truth, yet wonder what its applications may be. When you bring forth an incident from actual experience, their attention is renewed and their faces lighten. "Ah, now I see," each says to himself.

Many of us preachers at some time or other while attempting to impress the importance of the Church upon the hearers have said that people would not live in a churchless town. Perhaps even in the utterance there was some slight misgiving—was that statement more of hope than of assurance? As we left the pulpit, we were wondering how convincing that statement really had been. Dr. Charles R. Brown uses the following story in a slightly different connection in a sermon entitled "Move On." If we had used it to fortify the statement of the necessity of the Church, all doubts would have vanished:

"Forty-six years ago a man, who was bitterly opposed to religion in every form, acquired a large fortune by mining operations in the State of Montana. These facts were given me at that time by an officer of the Presbyterian Home Missionary Society who had been keenly interested in the experiment. The man decided to use his fortune in starting there a community which would be thoroughly and ideally secular. He purchased a thousand acres of land on the railroad in a beautiful part of the state and had it laid out as a townsite. Paved streets, sewers, water, and gas were installed. He built schoolhouses and a hospital, a theater, a dance hall, and a clubhouse. He established parks and playgrounds. He built a lot of attractive homes which could be purchased on very easy terms. He started at his own expense a number of industrial and commercial enterprises which could be bought with a clear prospect of profit. He provided securely against the introduction of his pet aversion, religion, by having inserted in all deeds to land sold a reversionary clause, stating that if the property should ever be sold or leased for any religious purpose whatsoever, the title should at once revert to the original owner. This made it impossible for any branch of the Church to establish there a place of worship. Then, by generous advertising, he invited the public to come and settle in this ideal place.

"In the course of a few years, he gathered a population of four or five thousand people, attracted by the beauty of the situation, the financial opportunities, and the sheer novelty of it. It was difficult from the start to get decent women to come in any considerable number—the other kind came and plied their trade without let or hindrance. The saloons were not curbed in any way, and they did a thriving business in that frontier town. But high-minded parents were reluctant to select that place as a suitable location in which to bring up their children. Children were scarce, and it was hard for the public schools to get the right sort of young women to teach the children who were there.

"The experiment continued for about five years, when the bottom seemed to drop out of everything and the man feared that the whole layout would be thrown back upon his hands as a bankrupt concern. He therefore published in the papers and by handbills this 'Manifesto,' which was a curious mixture of mental incongruity and irreverence:

" 'TO WHOM IT MAY CONCERN

" 'God knows that there is no such person as God, and my motto has always been, "To Hell with Religion."

" 'But for some fool reason, which no man can fathom, I have found by experience that we cannot do business in this country on any other basis than that silly bit of sentiment which we stamp on our coins, "In God we trust."

" 'Therefore, infernal foolishness though it all is, I have sent out for a parson and we are going to build a Church.'

"And that was the end of his diverting experiment." [31]

All the preachers of the ages who have been effective in their messages have known this power of incident and event told in story form. And wise is the preacher today who early in his ministry learns the exacting art of story-telling. It is an art worth all the effort it costs to learn.

HISTORY LIVING ANEW

People are interested in other people, what they do, and why. Because a person lived a thousand or three thousand years ago is no reason that he is uninteresting to a present-day congregation. If any historical scene is dramatically presented, hearers become concerned. All the pages of history, both secular and religious, are open to the minister. Events, characters, historical scenes from past life and from the Bible are ever ready to enrich the presentation of truth.

VARIETIES OF ILLUSTRATIONS

Two requirements are necessary to make historical characters or events suitable for pulpit usage. The first is that it is apropos, fits into the present scene, and actually illustrates the thought. This, of course, should be true of every illustration, of whatever kind it may be—it should illustrate.

The second is that the person presented or the scene recreated becomes a living, vital being. Often, especially in material taken from the Bible, the event is so familiar to the congregation that when it is mentioned, the people feel that they already know all about it. Whenever the preacher mentions any event with which the congregation is even remotely familiar, they close their ears to any presentation of it. The preacher is often forced into the position of an old colored man who was bemoaning the new generation of youth, "Yo' cain't tell 'em nuthin'. When yo' tells 'em anything, it's done already knowed."

The opposite danger needs to be given consideration. The preacher is so thoroughly familiar with a certain passage that he is sure it is known by the congregation. He feels that a casual reference or allusion will bring the entire event before the congregation. He forgets that, while the people of today consider themselves well informed, most of them know practically nothing about the Bible.

In both these situations, but especially where the events are familiar to the congregation, the preacher must recast or retell the experiences with new insight and new life. This takes imagination, and controlled imagination must be allowed full reign.

If in his study the minister will read and reread the passage, get all the outside help from commentaries and historical studies; then, in imagination put himself in that ancient day, dress himself in ancient clothes, see the physical setting, note the unusual customs and costumes, the racial or temporary characteristics, especially the peculiar and unusual ones of each person which make him a distinct personality; recreate the conversation; enter for himself into the characters; re-live the scene, and then put that person or event which he would describe into the best language of which he is capable, his sermon will leap into vital being. His congregation will find new life from the Scriptures or from the lives and history of mankind.

In this connection the preacher will study the methods and art of the great Biblical preachers, past and present. In the modern short thirty-minute sermon the method of presentation will be somewhat different, more graphic and less verbose. The preacher's study of the masters will not be to reproduce their word pictures, but to learn the methods through which he may become such an artist as to make the people of a bygone age walk and talk from his own pulpit.

With what consummate skill Dr. Charles R. Brown can paint a Scriptural scene of crisis and moral retribution! The sermon is entitled "I Am Joseph," and is largely a recital of the life of Joseph—yet you continually feel as though the events were taking place now, and somehow your own soul is involved.

"Joseph knew them, but they did not know him in this strange guise of an Egyptian official.

"After various devices, by which he tested their feeling for their father and for his younger brother, Benjamin, son also of the favorite wife, he decided to make himself known to them. 'Cause every one to go out,' he said to his attendants. He was left there alone with those brothers who years before had done him the wrong. Now, not as a boy helpless in their hands, not lying at the bottom of a pit, where they had cast him before selling him as a slave, but as a high official standing close to the throne of Pharoah, he said to them in their own tongue, 'I am Joseph, your brother, whom ye sold into Egypt.'

"What a striking situation! What an outcome for all those processes of even-handed justice which had been at work! What a vindication for one whose life had been characterized by integrity, purity, kindliness! What a day of judgment upon the wrongdoing of ten selfish, cruel men!

"The guilty men looked up into the face of him whom they had wronged, not knowing what the next hour might bring. Oriental despots usually cut off the heads of those who opposed their wills. Standing there in that foreign court, the ten brothers were even more helpless than the boy had been when they sold him to the Midianites. It was a time of heart-searching when this richly apparaled, powerful official looked down upon them, and in their own tongue, with accents painfully familiar to their astonished ears, said, 'I am Joseph, whom ye sold.' " [32]

There is one danger which perniciously creeps into such preaching. It is that the descriptive events of the days of the past shall occupy too large a part of the sermon. A modern sermon of about thirty minutes in length cannot contain an undue amount of description. The purpose of allowing the great and the small, the good and the bad characters of the past to pass before our people is that they may influence the living to shun the evil and cleave to the good. To avoid the extreme length of delineation, cultivate the art of impressionistic description. A bold touch, a suggestive phrase, an illuminative flash, a decisive word; these will throw the character into the center of the hearer's mind and his own imagination will fill in the details, probably much more rapidly than spoken words might do. A brief paragraph will often suffice.

"Selfish individualism for man or nation in this new world is downright insanity. . . . Bring this truth for a moment down to our individual consciences. Though Jeremiah was trying to save the Jewish people from their fate, his nephew Baruch—the private secretary who preserved the records of his ministry—was tempted to a selfish individualism. Member of a great family, with as good a chance as any one to serve his private ambition, he saw his own brother achieve political prestige and was tempted to a selfish life. Then Jeremiah, seeing how desperately critical the social situation was, challenged him with words that I wish could be burned into the conscience of this country: 'Seekest thou great things for thyself? Seek them not.' " [33]

70

VARIETIES OF ILLUSTRATIONS

I once heard an archeologist, whom one would expect to be as dry as the dust on a mummy, deliver several of the most interesting sermons which I have ever had the privilege of hearing. He so vividly recreated the events of the Scriptures that the congregation at the conclusion found themselves suddenly aware that they were living in the twentieth century and yet feeling of a certainty that those ancient people were their contemporaries. It is an art greatly to be coveted—and one which yields largely to experimentation and labor.

History in the Making

We pass from the history of the past to history in the making, events which take place about us continually and become the stuff out of which will be made the history books of tomorrow. There are daily scenes, personal experiences, events of the times, from the song of a redbird to the clash of mighty armies. Multimillioned are the happenings about us, hot with life and drama, full of human interest, joy, and despair, out of which the preacher may find material for the following Sunday's discourse. The variety in the present-day world is too diversified and too vast to attempt to outline.

Jesus and the preachers before our century had only that which came to hand, a few books, conversation with others about them, a bit of travel, and that was all. How times have changed! The death of a saintly priest on a leper isle in mid-Pacific is instant news in the humblest and farthest village. When the newspaper, magazines, flood of books, and the radio bring to every preacher the world and its daily

71

happenings, how can a man go into his pulpit with little or no illumination in his sermons? Living in a world tremendous with vast human upheavals in personal, social, and religious realms, the man in the pulpit is surrounded with materials to make the message walk down the aisles and stand before each hearer in flesh and blood. Few men have lived in an era so changing and cataclysmic; no men before us ever had the chance to know what was happening to their day, as we, by a thousand daily means, can know what takes place, not only in the capitals of the world but in the farthest and plainest hamlet.

From his own personal experiences, his own history, the minister may cull those illustrations which will contribute much to the vitality and freshness of his ministry. These may be gleaned from his own life, from his pastoral visitation, from the assembled congregation, from the example of people of his own or his member's acquaintance.

Any personal experience, as an illustration, must be truthful. Or should that be said to ministers? It ought not to be necessary except that in many places ministers have the reputation of exaggeration in regard to the stories they tell, particularly personal ones. We need to hold the confidence of our people. No personal recital knowingly should pass our lips exaggerated or untrue!

And yet these personal events, if well told and in due modesty, will provide a variety of illustrative material as wide as the many people and experiences which the minister is able to command. How homely is this illustration told by

Dr. Merton S. Rice: "I sat on Christmas eve listening to my radio. I believe I have never before heard jazz at its worst so crashingly done from almost every station. Suddenly, by the very slightest shift of the finder, I caught the truly wonderful melody of a great choir singing in all the sweeping impressiveness of 'The Messiah.' I held it against all the jazz in the world." [84]

WITHOUT A PARABLE SPAKE HE NOT

It is an interesting commentary that Jesus hardly ever spoke except in connection with a parable and that modern preachers hardly ever use one. In the Scriptural sense a parable was a story, either of an event or of an imaginary nature, a story true to life, but which possibly or even probably did not occur. Jesus filled his hearers' minds with them and, strange as it seems, present-day preachers rarely, if ever, present truth in this manner.

Preachers seldom have the opportunity of hearing other ministers preach; but if that has been your privilege, or you read sermons often, when have you had given to you a message through parable? And more pointedly, when have you presented your truth in the most Scriptural method, by parable?

Presumably parables are rare because most preachers are incapable of inventing them. It is indeed an unusual intellect which can grasp a profound truth and present it in an appealing picture. And yet the failure of modern preachers to use this method of parable for fear they are not capable, reminds one of the track athlete, a senior in college, who, being proficient in several races, was called upon during his teammate's illness to represent his school in the low hurdles race. He had never tried this event before; but, forced into the situation, he did the best he could. It was soon discovered that in this particular dash he had talents which might have made him a champion, except that, being a senior, his career was about over. Even though parabolic teachings are so rarely used today, is there not the same justification for them that there was in the Old and New Testament times?

Dr. Paul W. Quillian delivered a message on "The Church and the World Crisis" to five thousand young people gathered at the Methodist Young People's Conference in Memphis. His analogy of the Church to a modern, efficient service station, which provided fuel, replacements for worn-out parts, preventive care that all working mechanism was performing faithfully and safely, wrecker and repair service, will not soon be forgotten by those young people. "Now no parable is complete enough," he said, "to cover adequately so large a subject as the Church and its varied functions; but I hold up before you tonight the interesting parable of the service the Church of Jesus Christ can render. God's service station is the Church. Surely that is a function of the Church of Jesus Christ. Wrecks of personalities do need to be reclaimed. Road information in the midst of times like these needs to be given. Preventive work, that our journey may be made safer, is certainly needed. And best of all, dynamic

74

that shall provide energy for us to continue on the journey of our life needs to be given." [35]

A cultivation of this method of presenting truth, even though used only occasionally, would be well worth attempting and would provide for the congregation at least once in a while a message which would not be forgotten so quickly. "Of all the public instructions of our Lord Jesus Christ, the only perfect preacher that ever lived, a very large proportion, probably more than one-half of all that are recorded, were delivered in the form of comparison or parable." [36] This phase of the art of preaching is worth striving to master. If the short story writer gives ample time to learning the technique of his art, why should the preacher not attempt early in his ministry to master the parabolic method of preaching?

HUMOR AND SARCASM

Here are two means which will either greatly help the preacher or may destroy his message in part or entirely— humor and sarcasm. To some people is given the gift of humorous expression, some few attain to proficiency in bringing laughter to others, and many are the pitiable failures who attempt but never achieve. One who possesses a keen perception of the humorous has an asset which, when rightly used, puts barbs on his thoughts. There is small place for jokes in the pulpit, but the man who can put humorous twists to thought which bring a smile to the mind even if the lips do not move is the most fortunate speaker of all.

Dr. Stanley Jones enlivened and projected his message

immeasurably when at several points he used instances like the following: Speaking upon the general uncertainty of the times he related this instance: "A Chinese father was enrolling his son in school. Upon the application blank for admission was a question asking the religion of the student. The father wrote, 'Religion? . . . Confusion!'" Dr. Jones was again indicating the unity of the Gospel. He said the social Gospel was like the body and the individual Gospel like the soul of that body. The individual Gospel alone is a ghost and the social Gospel by itself is a corpse. Later he said that the universality of religion is apparent to all except a few who are locally minded. He said, "Two plus two equal four. That is universal. Two plus two equal five. That is local."

Here is an incident that is quite usable. It is not a joke, but has a sharp point. "A man got off the train for a few moments at a Southern station, saw an old Negro to whom he put the question, 'Uncle, do you find anyone around here enjoying religion?' The old darkey quietly replied, 'Them's as got it is.'"

If humor is used merely to court favor, to entertain, to display cleverness, it is entirely out of place. But if it throws light upon the subject, it is most valuable.

"The Spiritual Basis of Security" is a sermon theme in which Dr. M. S. Rice uses this instance:

"There appeared in the papers a very interesting item on the rugged character of General von Hindenburg shortly after his death. He typified our self-confident age, but he is now symbolic in the collapse of his confidence. A group of newspaper reporters were interviewing him, and one of them as spokesman for the company said: 'All your life, General, you have been a man of iron will and self-control. We would like to ask you for the secret of that fact, and to inquire, for the help it may be to others, what do you do when you feel yourself getting nervous?'

" 'I whistle,' replied the great German.

" 'But, sir, none of us had ever heard you whistle.'

" 'Is it possible?' replied the man of iron will, with feigned surprise. 'Now that I come to think about it, neither have I.' " [37]

In regard to sarcasm, here certainly is variation from the routine, but it is frequently the last fortress before defeat. One who must rely upon sarcasm to carry his point has chosen the frailest weapon with which to fight. It is keen as a rapier thrust when used at the right moment, and when it comes from a man of deep sympathy and is prefaced or followed by humor, it may carry the charge of the day.

DESCRIPTION

The preacher continually calls upon himself to describe some scene or setting, some person or group, some character or mental state. How easy it is to say too much and how difficult to depict with accuracy and vividness, briefly.

The illustration of Dr. Brown about the churchless town (quoted page 64) might be more briefly stated, and yet it was necessary to show the attractiveness of the community without the church in order to indicate its essential necessity.

The art of picturing briefly as well as imaginatively the ancient scene in terms of the modern is shown in the sermon, "How to Face Life with Steady Eyes," by Dr. Arthur John Gossip. "There was consternation in Jerusalem. For days ugly rumors had been blowing in on every wind. . . . Then the first panting refugees arrived, with hideous stories, exaggerated no doubt by their panic, of what was happening below the horizon yonder. And by and by the roads were blocked by fleeing folk."

Then he connects the fleeing folk of long ago with present-day brothers in distress: "Once I rode up for two days through the like in France. Never a male there younger than seventy; mile after mile of hurrying women, and children pleasantly excited, poor innocents, and old tottering men, each of them, to the feeblest and the weest, loaded with bundles of cherished possessions, and all of them dry-eyed, big-hearted, still unbroken, although leaving everything they had and knew, and faring forth into a homeless, empty, hopeless world." [38]

POETRY

It is doubtful whether a man has a place in the pulpit who is not a poet. By this is not meant one who can rhyme phrases and cast his thought into measured cadences of speech, but one who knows that deeper poetry which collects all the reality of daily life into its vaster interpretation. To Jesus all the life of nature, lilies and sparrows, a lost coin and a swept house, a robbed traveler and a blind beggar, were gathered into the symphony of God. To all real preachers life in its fullness of expression, its human degradation, and its divine aspiration, gathers into the rhythm of poetry.

No one is closer to the preacher than the poet. He sees behind the outward expression to the inward reality. He has that kinship with the spiritual and the divine. And in language that only he can command he paints the ineffable glories of the spirit or the haunting wretchedness of want or the undying dream of a peaceful and warless earth. One of the most powerful allies of the preacher is this brother, the poet.

By observation as well as by the testimony of others, I can testify that whenever a preacher quotes well an apt poem, the interest of the congregation immediately quickens. Love and the poet will be the preacher's means of encircling the globe with the interracial, intersocial, and international gospel of the Christ who knew no boundaries, class, or caste. While the average person does not read much poetry, there is a universal liking for the rhythmic and beautiful which can only be expressed in verse.

Poetry not only gives variety, but it adds point. Often a poem brings to focus an idea more beautifully and powerfully expressed than could any combination of words in prose or any other type of illustration.

In the following, poetry is not used merely to have lovely verses in the message, but each brings to a focus the idea of that section. The message is on prayer, and the points are as follows:

I. *Urging a consideration of prayer in the growth of the Christian life:*

> "Each night my bonny sturdy little lad
>   Persists in adding to his 'Now I lay me'
> This earnest little plea,
>   'God make me big.'
> And I his mother do echo
>   In a contrite heart,
> 'God make me big.'" [39]

II. *How prayer meets the needs of each individual soul:*

> "My problems are so great today,
>   There is a room where I must go
> And close the door, and kneel and pray,
>   And only God shall know.
>
> A room where often I have knelt
>   And agonized, and prayed, and plead,
> Until, all comforted, I felt
>   God's hand upon my head.
>
> A room I seek when I am glad
>   To thank the Giver of it all.
> Without Him I would not have had
>   These joys I have, at all.
>
> Within my house is one small room,
>   A haven from distress and care.
> I turn to it—and through the gloom
>   Seek God, and find Him there." [40]

III. *How intercessory prayer meets the needs of others:*

"The day was long, the burden I had borne
　　Seemed heavier than I could longer bear,
And then it lifted, but I did not know
　　Someone had knelt in prayer,

Had taken me to God that very hour,
　　And asked the easing of the load, and He,
In infinite compassion, had stooped down
　　And taken it from me.

We cannot tell how often as we pray
　　For some hurt one, bewildered and distressed,
The answer comes—but many times those hearts
　　Find sudden peace and rest.

Someone had prayed, and Faith, a reaching hand,
　　Took hold of God, and brought Him down that day!
So many, many hearts have need of prayer—
　　Oh, let us pray!" [41]

SYMPHONIC SERMONS

There is a poetic method of preaching that has proved valuable and effective. It has been emphasized most emphatically by Dr. William Stidger. This type of message has been called "The Symphonic Sermon." In it the preacher links up the text with a two-line couplet and at the close of each major point or primary illustration repeats those two lines until he has sung them into the memory of the people.

Here are a few paragraphs from a sermon of my own on

"Men Like Mountains," in which the text is "I have fought a good fight, I have finished my course, I have kept the faith." [42]

"There is an enlightening illumination in that greatest of all Lincoln poems, 'Lincoln, the Man of the People,' by Edwin Markham. Two lines in it have flashed into my mind a picture of Lincoln that I shall never forget.

"Markham, the author, is one of those mystic poets with unusual vision who sees God's purpose in all the universe, in nature, and in man. He sees the mountains in purple majesty as symbols of the eternal hills. He finds something of grandeur in mountains towering heavenward that thrills and enchants the souls of men. They stand as symbols of cloud-topped eternal values.

"He can stand on the shore of an ocean and feel the surging restlessness of the beating seas. Their untiring, everlasting surging tugs at his soul. The mountains and the seas symbolize more than any other features of the earth its greatness and its power. With the realization of this greatness in his mind Markham flashed out that lightning illumination of the character of Lincoln:

'Here was a man to hold against the world,
A man to match the mountains and the sea.'

"God in His majesty and power can make mountains and seas, but He can also make a man to match them."

The poetic melody of the above couplet repeats itself several times:

"These individuals of whom we have been thinking have been those who have lived in fields we think of as secular and yet the essence of religion has been among them all. Let us now call to mind those who stand above the valleys of life as towering giants because they are outstandingly religious. There is Moses, the mighty lawgiver, rising above the ancient world. There are the prophets, men of God, who devoted themselves to leading the people to higher conceptions of God and life—and many of whom gave their lives in payment for their pains. There, transcending all the rest, is Jesus, towering upward as the Son of God, giving his life to win a world to God, his Father, giving his all even to death upon the cross.

> 'Here were men to hold against the world,
> Men to match the mountains and the sea.' "

The sermon concludes, "May your life be worthy of such an epitaph as this:

> 'Here was a man to hold against the world,
> A man to match the mountains and the sea.' "

This method not only fascinates a congregation, but leaves the truth and the text hammered home. I once preached on co-operation in the Church, using two lines from Kipling's *Jungle Book*. Several months later a woman said to me, "I shall never forget those two lines in the sermon on co-operation,

'The strength of the wolf is the pack
And the strength of the pack is the wolf,'

nor shall I forget the text, 'By this shall all men know that ye are my disciples, if ye love one another.' "

This method may not appeal to all preachers; yet if used with sincerity and not for sensation, it is a powerful weapon. Two such couplets with intriguing value are:

"When the fight begins within himself,
A man's worth something." [43]

"I could not love thee, dear, so much,
Loved I not honor more." [44]

We shall come in due time to discussing how best to use poetry and the other windows in our sermons.

FLASHES OF ILLUMINATION

On some occasion, perhaps an exceptionally rare one, there comes to you a fitting and dramatic illustration that was never before on land or sea. It is your own, original, a flash of genius, like an angel strain in the night. When it comes, seize it at once before it elusively escapes.

Dr. John Timothy Stone is preaching on "Divine Power through Human Agency," and concludes with this brilliant insight:

"In concluding our thought I see before me an all-powerful dynamo, charged with power beyond the comprehension of man. It fills a vast space upon my right. Upon my left I see tens of thousands of cities, villages, yes, and distant continents as well as countries multiplied, which reach into the millions— the unnumbered inhabitants of a world. This vast world needs controlling motion, the use of power, light, warmth, heat—factories, shops, stores, homes, vast buildings, tiny closets, great schools, small homes—all kinds and conditions of men in multiplied associations, business, commerce, transportation, domesticity, and individuality. This immense dynamo can serve and fulfill the requirements of all complicated needs and activities of this vast cosmopolitan throng and set all wheels in motion. A cable reaches out from these needs of men to the left, to the great dynamo. There is the need of a connection between that cable and this immense dynamo of divine strength. That connection is found in the human element, in man.

"Jesus Christ, the Son of God, has made possible the use and control of that Infinite Dynamo's power and connects that power with human need through his Son, Jesus Christ. He left us his Spirit. That divine power becomes the possession of human life, according to the power that worketh in us.' " [45]

A preacher can never afford to wait for these rare visitations. He must seek his illustrations in less dramatic moments, often by arduous search and careful preparation. These rare flashes of illumination come best and more often because of practice in the eternal pursuit of the fitting and proper illustration of a homelier nature.

Again there are sufferings so dire, wickedness so appalling, that public words must not touch them—yet somehow they must be uttered. There may be occasions when public feeling runs so high, emotions are so volatile, that frank statement is impossible. In such an hour wise is the St. John who can impeach his age and vision the Holy City with images which are foolishness to the worldly-wise and yet windows of heaven to the faithful!

THE DISPLAY ROOM

As we have visited the Display Room of Sermonic Windows we have seen a tiny aperture where a single word lets in a bright pencil of light. We have passed by the small openings of simile and metaphor and viewed the infinite variety of story windows through which pours the radiance from across the centuries, light from inspired men and women, heated events of history, pithy scenes of present-day living. We have noted the art glass windows of poetry with their delicate colors of varying emotions. We have seen the skylight through which at night the lightning of illuminated imagination flashes the miracle of heaven's fervent truth.

Here in the Show Room are the samples from which we may choose the particular windows for next Sunday's or next month's sermon. Variety everywhere, waiting only our selection.

> "Let there be many windows in your soul
> That all the glory of the universe
> May beautify it." [46]

IV

GATHERING MATERIALS: EXPERIENCE AND OBSERVATION AS A SOURCE

W HERE can I find illustrations for my sermons?" asked a young preacher. He was but repeating what preachers everywhere, older ones as well as younger, are continually inquiring.

The answer may be taken from our analogy of windows. The materials which go into their manufacture come from widely separated places, from the pines of Georgia, or the oaks and spruce of the North woods, from the iron deposits of Pennsylvania, the glass-producing cliffs along the Mississippi, to which are added lead, paint, and chemicals brought together from many different localities. Depending upon the kind of window and its expected use, materials are sought from whatever place most readily yields to such a demand.

Materials for windows in sermons come from as wide sources. Their selection depends as well upon the kind of illustrations the preacher would construct and the use to which they are to be put.

Once I asked a preacher of long experience, who was skilled in the art of illustration, where he secured his materials. He looked at me somewhat in dismay, and I wondered whether his dismay was at my youthful ignorance or because that question was not easily answered. He replied, "Where do I get my illustrations? Oh, everywhere!" This was not much of an answer to me then, but during the years since it has grown increasingly meaningful. When one hears the best sermons or reads them as preachers must, it is to discover that the great preachers have indeed wandered the world and brought back rare treasures from all places and peoples, from Nature in all her grandeur, and from every point of contact between the human mind and the world, both animate and inanimate.

Two Methods

There are two methods to pursue in this everlasting search for the right illustration, the direct and the indirect. The latter is the better although the former is quite necessary.

Every preacher realizes the necessity of seeking to find illustrative material for the sermon immediately at hand. That sermon for next Sunday morning must have cases in point and they must be sought out now. The calendar waits for no man. Delay is fatal. The task resolves itself into an effort to find a particular illustration for a certain place in a particular sermon. The skillful preacher in such a predicament will know how to marshal his forces to secure those instances which will suit his present purpose.

It is possible that in the moment of need there will come from out the deeps of a well-trained mind and a long life of experience enough or possibly more than enough incidents to fill the sermon in hand. It is out of this life filled to overflowing that the finest and best material comes. The immediately necessary exemplifications come best and more often by practice in the eternal search for the fitting and proper.

In conversation with a certain bishop he spoke about the illustrations used in his sermons. Unfortunately election to the episcopacy does not always guarantee such powerful and well-illustrated sermons as this bishop preaches. He said, "I never seek for illustrations in particular. When I need them, they seem to come from my reading and out of my experience with people." Here was a man equipped with a remarkable memory who was drawing upon the resources of a whole lifetime of intensive living with people and the great minds of literature. "Out of the Overflow" is what Dr. Stidger calls such preaching. It is like an artesian well, pouring forth from the depths of the hidden years.

"Paradoxically as it sounds, 'the less special preparation that is needed for a sermon, the better the sermon is.' Someone humorously said that the only way to preach well is to begin ten years ago." [1]

It is all-important to the young minister that he spend much of his time in getting ready for that overflow in later years. Hours of daily study and multiplied human contacts, not primarily for their present dividends, but for the enrichment of life, will produce long afterwards a finer contribution to the congregations to whom he shall preach. Out of a lifetime of careful observation, out of the overflow of full living, the best preaching will come.

"How did Dr. Fosdick become the great preacher he is? By the hardest kind of work, unceasing, laborious toil, painstaking industry. For thirty years, approximately, since the days of his first pastorate in Montclair, New Jersey, he has spent the mornings of five days a week in his study. No messages get to him there, no telephone calls can reach him, no visitors are admitted. In such seclusion, he 'toils terribly' over his sermons. This long practice, self-discipline, persistent purposeful life program, is the answer to the question, How did Fosdick become the great preacher he is?" [2]

A young minister must face two questions. Not having lived my life as yet, where may I, as a beginner, find enough for next Sunday's sermons? And how may I go about filling my life with sufficient to overflow in the years to come? To answering these pertinent questions we will now give our attention.

THE "WINDOW" MIND

People who attend a Fair or an Exposition see that which they intend to see. The farmer sees hogs, the machinist visits the mechanical arts building, and all of us are found gazing covetously at the latest automobiles. Each person looks for and is attracted to that which is of real interest to him.

Likewise, the preacher who is continually preparing sermons becomes increasingly alert to those incidents and events which will help him to present his message most interestingly and forcefully. This is often called the "homiletic mind," where one's attention not only naturally but by active interest is directed to anything and everything which will give point to sermons—and also proves helpful to occasions of personal spiritual counseling. As a builder of sermons you will have such an interest in everything and everybody for a possible place in your messages.

The answer to the question, "Where shall I find illustrations for my sermons?" is still the same: Everywhere. The ways by which men search may be as infinite and as varied as individual preachers, but one fact remains: Every pastor who becomes a successful preacher is everlastingly at the task of gathering and assimilating illustrative material.

SEARCH THE SCRIPTURES

To some preachers it may appear trite to state that the Bible is the principal source of sermonic illustrations, and to others, who feel the urge of the modern, it may appear that more contemporary sources should have primary place. This latter attitude may be largely due to the fact that the Scriptural material has, entirely too often, been used in a stereotyped manner. Between these poles of opinion is a vital use of the Bible as the living power of the sermon.

There are innumerable descriptions and delineations of more than passing interest in *The Use of the Bible in Preaching,* by Carl S. Patton. There is something intriguing about this description of one of the better-known characters of the Old Testament:

91

"Saul is a sad instance of a man who was never equal to his job. He was chosen for his size and good looks—'head and shoulders above the rest of the people.' Some wit has said, 'All men are equal—from the neck down.' Even that is not quite true. But the main advantage of any man over another lies in what is above the shoulders. And it was there that Saul was weak. Moody, irresolute, suspicious, alternating quickly between fits of bravery and of cowardice, 'unstable in all his ways,' as James says, he was marked for failure from the start. For only a few months his star ascended, then hung for a moment in the sky, and began to decline." [3]

The Bible is the "greatest picture book in print," the truthful and tested record of life experiences. Even its prose is lyric in its figures. Its resources are inexhaustible and, because of the sacred associations which cluster around them, it has power to persuade which is absent from any other materials. While no other source is the equivalent, yet it can be used to the exclusion of current matter. People today desire to know if this life of Scripture can be practiced and under what modern circumstances.

The Bible has its value because it is always contemporary. Dr. S. Parkes Cadman, beside whom there has been no more powerful speaker to the issues of today, says: "Dissertations on current events and literary or other topics which have no religious realism in them are wearying to the worshiping soul. The corporate life of our Christian witness does not center in Homer, Dante, Shakespeare, or Milton, but in the Old and New Testament writings." [4] Wise is the preacher who, beginning early in his ministry and continuing unabated, derives all he can from the Sacred Writings of Christendom.

It is difficult to discuss the use of the Bible solely as illustrative material, as it is the chief source of all preaching. While there are admittedly lesser lights in other religions and derivative reflections in the Christian centuries since the Biblical days, the Bible is the central sun for our preaching. We search the Scriptures not only that we may have incidents and events from the divine record, but primarily to find there the vivid account of God and men in the terrific struggle against the forces of evil, forging out in that intense heat of living the refined gold which eternally abides. So it is no easy matter to discuss the central sun of preaching as though it were a satellite circling some more important body.

But apart from this larger use, the Bible may be, in the restricted sense in which we are now using it, the principal and most fruitful source of illustration.

Within the library of Scripture is every conceivable type of illustration on every subject or theme which the preacher shall touch. There are events of gripping intensity, pastoral scenes of surpassing beauty, ancient customs with modern counterparts and contrasts, institutions which reflect age-old but eternally new virtues and vices, stark Nature, red in tooth and claw but still with the dream shining through, and portraits of people with their motives and thoughts laid bare such as no book ever before or since has revealed them. Above all is the story of the Divine Man who is the center of the world to which these all belong, and who remains the center of the world to which we belong.

THE SCRIPTURES AT WORK

You may preach an entire sermon from some character, event, movement, developing idea, or story recorded in its pages. This lends a variety to the regular schedule which is always appreciated by the congregation. Frequent treatment of this kind is always rewarding.

Dr. Charles Reynolds Brown, of Yale Divinity School, has a sermon entitled "I Am Joseph!" [5] He begins with an arresting statement: "The main value of the Old Testament lies in the fact that it is a big, thick slice of human experience." In the next paragraph he proceeds with picturesque phrase to set the scene. "These Old Testament stories are well told. The men who put them in shape, as we find them, were artists—they had keen eyes for dramatic situations. Take this story of Joseph! . . ." He then proceeds to tell the story in gripping style so that with it as a background the events of today come to the forefront of the stage of action.

Dr. Patton takes a parable of Jesus which is recorded only in Mark. [6] In the introduction he says that perhaps Matthew and Luke did not copy this story from Mark, the only material not included in either one or both of them, because they thought it was too simple. He continues in the sermon, "For simple it certainly is. The farmer sows his seed. Then he sleeps, and rises night and day and lets it grow. He cannot even understand how it does grow. He only knows that it does. No use for him to worry about it. He cannot hurry it. All he can do is to watch it and gather the harvest when it is ripe. 'The Kingdom of God,' says Jesus, 'is like that.' If it is worth while for Jesus to say so simple a thing, it is probably worth while for us to see what is involved in it." [7]

Or again and constantly you will be using Scriptural material to illustrate individual and particular points in your sermons.

"A very suggestive revelation of human nature is given us in the Genesis story of Rachel, the young wife of Jacob. When her husband broke with her father and set out with his household from her native land, she went along, but she carried hidden in her saddle some of her father's household gods. She could not bring herself to make a clear-cut change from the idol-worshipers to the Jehovah-worshipers. Rachel's error was the same in principle as that of Lot's wife and that of many since her day. If we were to go out to the geographical frontiers of the Christian mission field, we should see many recruits coming over into the membership of the Christian Church carrying certain of their old pagan ideals and practices with them. But there is no need to go to Africa or China to see this phenomenon. We have it all about us." [8]

The most productive method of accumulating Scriptural material for preaching, both as the basis of an entire sermon and as illustrative of particular topics, is to be saturated in the Scriptures. Of course when you need a certain idea illustrated you will search the Bible until you find some character or event which brings out most forcefully your conviction. But the most productive method is to be saturated in the Scriptures, to read regularly that you *may be found out* by those persons and truths which will reveal themselves only when you have read about them again and yet again until, quite suddenly, as though by magic they leap from the printed page to become life and blood. An expository preacher of great power has advised that preachers should read the Bible through often with considerable rapidity in order to keep the settings freshly in mind; not with the idea of finding an illustration for the sermon of the present week, but that out of the overflow of a mind well filled the Scriptural illustrations will come unsought at the needed moment.

TELLING THE INCIDENT

Just another word about the telling of Scriptural incidents. There are many passages with which the congregation will be familiar. Such knowledge on their part is a distinct advantage. If you are certain of this familiarity, then paint the character of the person or the scene briefly with bold strokes and with imaginative insight into the historical situation. Bring that character or scene to life quickly and pointedly.

The event in which David, having defeated the enemy, comes back to the capital, dancing before the restored Ark of the Covenant, is probably well known to the average congregation. Dr. Patton brings the scene to startling reality.

King David had saved the ark. He "had righted an ancient

wrong. . . . It had been a great day. But there was one fly in the ointment. As the procession moved past David's house there was a woman looking out of a window. It was Michal, his wife. Michal was the daughter of Saul. It is a hard matter to be the daughter of one king and the wife of another one who is supplanting him. Michal stood by David. When her father's soldiers came to his house to kill him, she helped him get away. She played her part as a dutiful wife in all the quarrels between him and her father. But it must have been a strain on her just the same.

"She loved her husband. But I suppose there were some things about him that she didn't like. It is often so. And the more a woman loves her husband, the more she is troubled by the things she does not like in him. Michal looked at David, as the procession came up the street, and saw him dancing like a dervish, with nothing on but a linen apron, and, says the writer, 'She despised him in her heart.' Poor David—what is the use of being king, what is the use of bringing home an ark, what is the use of anything, if your wife despises you?" [9]

However, it is seldom safe to take for granted that the congregation knows very much about the Bible. Such a revelation as was made by a questionnaire in Virginia among some 18,000 high school students, revealing that about 13,000 could not name three Old Testament prophets and that about 10,000 did not know the names of the four Gospels, does not indicate that there is more ignorance in Virginia than elsewhere, but that such a condition probably prevails in your community and in mine. To prevent falling into the trap of over-expectancy a preacher will do well to present the Bible as freshly and as vividly as possible, so that one familiar with it may see it in new perspective and one to whom it is unknown may see the living reality of that ancient event as though it were contemporary.

You cannot plagiarize from the Bible. Use all that you can as illustration for a twofold purpose: that you may increase among your congregation familiarity with the source of our religion and that you may have the most valid authority for your preaching.

RANGE THE WORLD AND THE AGES

There is open to the preacher of today a world of fascinating interest which no preacher before him ever entered. As he travels over the past, he not only has the Scriptures but also the life of bygone ages described and depicted as never previously. He may now study the great men and movements of history from a much more penetrating viewpoint. The old view of history chronologically recorded the dates, men, battles, dynasties. One who had a facile memory for statistics could major in history. But the new view pays little attention to the calendar except as it expresses the life forces which have made man; the social and political movements; the causes, effects, and forces in which the captains and the kings are often but pawns in the ongoing march of humanity.

Out of his study of the men and movements of the Christian Church, the preacher will be able to bring valuable help to men and women who today struggle and aspire that the Church Militant may become the Church Triumphant.

Not only the history of the Church, but also the world drama of all nations and all peoples, ancient as well as modern, yield their stories to make graphic the sermon. Where is the line between the religious and the secular? There are no events in which men are free from any motivation that is not selfish or unselfish, which does not affect the very destiny of souls in the making. With a world in turmoil from the fact that it does not see that its every action and its future is dependent upon moral choices, the preacher must find from history the sources of action, the motives of men, so that he can speak with assurance. When a man has the wide, understanding background which comes from knowledge of the entire life of nations and eras, he can relate a particular event or refer to a certain fact with much more intelligence, sincerity, and authority.

Dr. Lynn Harold Hough, one of the most widely read, scholarly, and brilliant preachers of this generation, said in a sermon on "Teachers and Disciples": "A few years ago I was traveling on the Mediterranean with a young British chemist, who, after completing his work at two technical schools, had spent three years at the University of Oxford. 'And what did Oxford do for you?' I asked him one day as we walked the deck of the little ship looking down at the sapphire sea. 'What did Oxford do for you after all your scientific training?' Very quietly and very thoughtfully he replied: 'Oxford taught me that science is a part of something larger than itself.' So a twentieth-century lad reached his hand across the centuries to grasp the hand of Aristotle." [10]

One thing is always apparent about the preaching of Dr. Hough and it is that he has reached a hand in every direction across centuries and continents and races of men, and what he says has the rich background of the timeless and universal. And so may every preacher reach his hand across the ages to make friends with all races, colors, and creeds.

THE EVENT OF THE MOMENT

Flooding from the newspapers and periodicals and over the radio come the mass of details out of which the historian of the future will cull the characters and movements which have made our times. Men, women, and youth flash upon the page for a moment and are gone—but are they? Each leaves his imprint, for good or ill, and history moves on. Great personages pass by, and others whose names are never remembered but who exhibit those qualities which make for the kingdom of God on earth,

> "A picket frozen on duty—
> A mother starved for her brood, . . .
> And millions who, humble and nameless,
> The straight, hard pathway plod." [11]

In that newspaper you read this morning are enough incidents to fill any sermon with contemporaneous and fervent living. Here is an Associated Press item picked out one morning by chance:

"Stranded in mid-air for hours by dense fog which swept in suddenly from the ocean and wiped out all landmarks, aviators of fourteen naval planes were safe on the ground today as a result of dramatic rescue and their own daring skill.

"Twenty-two planes from North Island Naval air station were aloft at dusk yesterday participating in Naval Day maneuvers when the fog swept in unexpectedly. Eight of them raced immediately to landing fields, but the others were caught in the swiftly forming impenetrable blanket.

"Four planes crashed, one of them bursting into flames, as twelve pilots dived blindly through the fog. But the greatest injury to any of the men was a sprained finger.

"By 8 P.M., two hours after the fog had swept in, only two planes were aloft.

"The two remaining ships were guided to safety by a transport pilot and 2,500 motorists summoned by radio to line the abandoned Camp Kearney airport and transform it with their headlights into a blazing field of light.

"Naval officials estimated they had only enough gasoline left to stay up 20 minutes longer."

For the purpose of a sermon the next to the last paragraph might be better used as follows (preserving absolutely the integrity of the facts): Suddenly there went out over the radio this message, "All automobile owners go to the landing field outside San Diego. Two fliers are lost in the fog and your going may help them to land." Soon the roads approaching the field were crowded with cars creeping through the inky blackness, hardly able to see with their feeble lights. As the cars arrived the authorities lined them up around the field with the cars facing inward. More than twenty-five hundred of them completely surrounded the landing ground. The word was passed around, "All lights on!"

The lights on no single car made much impression upon that night and fog, but the lights of two thousand five hundred of them lighted the field so brightly that a transport pilot could go aloft and guide the two aviators down to safety.

What an illustration for Christian co-operation! Neither your light nor mine is very bright, but if each and all would focus the light we have upon this world with its fog of sin and distress, then it would be so bright that our master Pilot, Christ, could go aloft and bring every lost soul to a safe landing.

Blessed are ye if ye see in the daily press more than the march of Time!

The Contemporary Situation

In the history of preaching is constantly noted the keen ingenuity born of necessity, whereby the preacher finds his most pointed barbs of illustration arising from the urgency of the contemporary situation. The pressure of the particular struggle of the time in which he preached has caused the minister to select those Biblical, historical, or contemporary events which would most pointedly indicate the direction of truth and religious hope. Whenever the preacher loses touch with the crisis of the present hour, he loses the ear of his time. Particularly have those led their own age who have shown eternal things through the windows of the present.

"How shall we think about God?" What a pertinent question! One which our age is anxiously seeking to have answered! Dr. Charles R. Brown faces the question squarely:

"Here we are in an orderly world! The heavens declare the glory of God and all these marvelous adaptations to varied forms of life show signs of intelligent handiwork. How did it all come about? 'By chance,' the lighthearted, lightheaded people say. Matter and force were here from the start—no one knows how—and it all just happened.

"You enter some great department store, Marshall Field's in Chicago or Wanamaker's in Philadelphia. You find on every side the evidence of order, method, purpose. Men's wear, women's wear, children's wear, furniture in one section and carpets in another, china in one section, notions in another, books, toys, games, all in place and all arranged with skill and taste! Who planned it? Nobody! There was no intelligence or purpose back of it. Matter and force, senseless atoms by some accidental maneuvering of themselves brought all that into existence as we see it.

"Stand in some great cathedral, Canterbury, Cologne, Chartres! Nave and transepts, choir and altar, lofty arches and flying buttresses, glorious stained glass and delicately carved wood! Who planned it? Nobody! It just happened. Matter and force, huge quarries of stone in yonder hillside

103

and the power of gravitation—somehow this stately cathedral took shape!

"We look out upon this marvelous universe, vaster, more majestic, more intricate than all the creations which have come from human hands and brains. Who planned and executed all this? How did it come about? When the lame, the halt, and the blind say, 'Nobody! There is neither intelligence nor purpose back of it,' it is to laugh. It does not make sense. The new physics taught by leading men of science, Millikan, Eddington, Jeans, puts another, profounder interpretation upon the world order. Swift as a thought our minds go back to those stately words, 'In the beginning, God created the heavens and the earth.' 'Before the mountains were brought forth, or ever thou hadst formed the earth and the world, even from everlasting to everlasting, thou art God.' Can anyone bring us a better hypothesis?" [12]

"Is our generation in its present serious difficulties partly at least because we too have tempted God by wanting the wrong things?" asks Dr. Charles W. Gilkey in a sermon on "Wishful Thinking in Religion." He thrusts this piercing quotation into the heart of that question: "The remark of Lincoln Steffens, as he looked out on the world to which another great war will bring irreparable disaster, points the same question, 'None of us wants war—but all of us want things that we cannot have without war.'" [13]

In the contemporary situation are social movements which will bear watching with that insight which comes alone to the SEER.

WHERE JESUS GOT HIS ILLUSTRATIONS

Would you interpret religion and life to the people as did Jesus? Then you would follow him into the realms where people live. Jesus got his illustrations from daily life, from life in the country and life in the city, outdoors and indoors. He spent his time out in Nature with an open mind. The lily and sparrow escaped his eye no more than they did the watchful care of his Father. Present-day "history," as most people will experience it, will be in the kitchen, behind the plow, operating a riveter, or playing with babies on the living room floor. If you can observe how people live daily and in what manner they are religious or "losing themselves from God," you will have the secret to their hearts. We *could make* history if we led our people to find the highest expression of living in the daily round of activities. It was there that Jesus found his most memorable illustrations. He never gave an illustration of a haggard-faced girl stuffing sausages into cans by the hour, because he never saw such a scene. But were he living today no trip to the stockyards would fail to impress him with the "human side of the news."

Dr. Halford Luccock has a way of penetrating our human inconsistencies and un-Christian acts of the present time through incidents gathered in the daily routine.

"An extreme instance of the same callousness of this Palestinian village (where there were those 'to whom he had become a familiar sight as a beggar'—John 9: 8) is that of a great architect, on the deck of a ferryboat in the Hudson River, when a stoker fell from the stern of a tug and was smashed by its screw to a pulp that left on the waters a lacquer of bloody oil. He merely cried, 'What color?' " [14]

Or again this insight: "In Arthur D. Howden Smith's life of John Jacob Astor, we read of the last act of Astor's life, signing the foreclosure of a mortgage. The name was affixed, and the pen dropped from the nerveless fingers. The ruling passion strong in death. 'Thou art what I get from life, O New York Real Estate!' " [15]

There are not many who see God more clearly in the contemporary scene, nor yet the weakness of our present undirected life.

"One Sunday in September more than six hundred thousand people paraded up and down the boardwalks of Coney Island.

"What a stupendous crowd! That is a larger number of people than engaged in all the crusades of Europe in the Middle Ages. It is a larger number of people than have gone out as missionaries of the Christian faith since the resurrection morning!

"What did such an enormous crowd mean? The answer can be given pretty largely in one word—*peanuts*. It meant nothing! That massive crowd walked up and down the thoroughfare eating peanuts and popcorn and went home again. It was not a crowd with any natural unity. It was not a crowd with any purpose. It was just a crowd.

"That crowd of over half a million is well worth thinking about in an age beset with the fundamental vulgarity of confusing the size of a thing with its significance." [16]

Let us add another incident of this keen observer about the art of observing: "Willa Cather has crept into many lives with understanding and sympathy. When only eight years old, on her father's Nebraska ranch, she would ride her pony round the country, getting acquainted with her polyglot neighbors—Swedes, Danes, Norwegians, Bohemians, Germans, French Canadians. 'I used to ride home,' she says, 'in the most unreasonable state of excitement. I always felt as if they told me so much more than they said—as if I had actually got inside another person's skin.' " [17]

Ah! That is it! "Getting inside another person's skin." When we can do that, we can begin to preach.

PERSONAL EXPERIENCES

Illustrations originating with the preacher are undoubtedly very effective. Any skilled preacher knows full well that there is a pickup in interest on the part of the congregation the moment the sermon moves into the realm of personal experience. There is power in the recital of an event in which Christ has motivated your own life or that of someone whom you know. Your own observation of people and affairs of the world are colored by the confidence placed in you as a prophet of God. A man is entirely justified in telling of his experiences in the Christian life. "Use that; in all modesty, but plainly and unaffectedly, without mock humility." [18]

There are four dangers to be assiduously avoided. One is that the recital should call more attention to the speaker than to the subject. Any illustration which leaves the "I" as the

107

final impression has no place in the sermon. The second is like unto it: that the sermon be made up too largely of a running commentary upon the minister's personal life, all the way from the new baby in the parsonage to his conversation in the barber shop. The preacher is important only as the mouthpiece of the truth. He is not the gospel. The third and opposite danger is as pernicious, that the preacher will feel too timid or falsely humble to present the incidents of his own life. The same test that will suit every illustration should be applied to those events of his own—namely, if it illustrates the point at issue, use it, frankly, without either false pride or mock humility. If it does not conform to this standard, reject it without further waste of time.

The fourth is the most hurtful and devastating danger of all, to enlarge, color, or heighten the effect so that the incident is exaggerated. The minister is so anxious that his point be proved that he gives every added weight possible to his story, enlarging here, adding a touch there, placing undue emphasis, or rewording the conversation to suit the point at issue until he has told what really never occurred. No end ever justifies this means. However good the intentions, it is no less than lying. Nothing will so destroy all that a minister says so much as telling one or two instances in such a way that the congregation knows they are exaggerated or never happened. The people demand sincerity of the man who represents the truth.

A father was telling an incident at a dinner table, so the story goes, after which his son asked, "Dad, is that true or were you just preaching?" Every time we tell some incident in the pulpit, let us pause before that boy—for he is in our congregation!

Pastoral Visiting

Every minister, whatever his geographical location or the size of his parish, is impressed as he visits among his people in their homes and at their work or as they come to him for consultation that here is a quarry where in struggle the people are working out the material of their lives, as well as the material for his sermons. In the hour when the white heat of suffering has purged away the dross, or a soul looks in faith out across an open grave, the minister sees the heroism so needed by others in his parish. When aspiring youths search intently through the modern ways of thinking and find stability for their ambitions in the Christ way, he knows of other young people who need that same guidance. As the rich man brings his two mites and the widow gives her all, he has in living flesh beheld the weakness of Mammon and the power of God. The man who with one hand holds to the promise of peace and with the other clings to a false nationalistic patriotism, brings to a crisis in the Armistice Day sermon the fundamental issue between a warless world and Armageddon. These daily contacts with his people bring to a focus the issues of living. Out of these circumstances within his own congregation in their occupations, home life, social and political attitudes, tragedies and victories, will come material to fill his sermons.

The minister will not go with a cold and heartless objectivity, as though here were cases to be dissected for his sermonic pleasure, but in the spirit of Christlike consecration to the sufferings and woes of his people, to share with them the winds of fortune and the hurricanes of disappointment. Because of his devoted compassion he will minister to these people, and out of such experiences he will find truth and hope for others of his flock who desperately need to know both the pitfalls of evil and the paths of righteousness. A minister devoted to his people will find abundant material to make his sermons realistic.

Dr. Daniel Poling writes this editorial tribute to one of the greatest of the American pulpit:

"S. Parkes Cadman was fighting for his life in an oxygen tent at Plattsburg as we sat down to write this month's news; before we'd written a dozen lines, the dreaded news came. The little boy from Shropshire who became the brightest star in the American ecclesiastical firmament had gone on. Cadman had lost his fight.

"I knew Dr. Cadman. Years ago, as a young minister, I sat in his Brooklyn study and complained to him that I had a lot of hypocrites in my congregation, and a lot of spiritual loafers. He looked at me with that famous Cadman twinkle in his eye and said: 'I know. I know. But if you want to help them and save yourself, you'll have to learn to love them, my boy.' That was all. That was enough.

"That, I think, was what made Cadman great: his capacity for love. He had a heart as big as Brooklyn, a mind that reached out for everybody. . . . But to me it wasn't his championship of Christian causes nor his cedar-like greatness that made him what he was; not that he was sought by every great pulpit in America and Europe. We'll forget that. But we can never forget that while he sat in the seats of the mighty, he never forgot the lowly. It was his common touch that made him so uncommon. Half the taxicab drivers in Brooklyn knew him, as a friend. He knew the newsboy on the corner by his first name, and all about his family; the cop on the corner was his intimate, and you'd better be careful when you talk to Pat about 'The Reverend.' The ash men, the boys in the firehouse down the street, clerks in candy stores, and motormen and doormen and millionaires and convicts: they knew this man and they loved him.

" 'Learn to love them, my boy.' I'll never forget his advice . . . nor him." [19]

Every incident which comes out of your own present or past congregation should be so changed in incidental details that no one can say, "I know of whom he is talking," or someone else can feel that his confidence has been betrayed. No member of the congregation should hesitate to come to see the minister because he is afraid that he could not trust his confidences longer than next Sunday.

"Betraying the Confessional" is the title of an article by Frances J. Nickels indicting the clergy with what is too often true. "I have been thinking back across the years of experience," she says. "How frequently we hear in pulpit, in public affairs, in classrooms, and in private conversation the most intimate confidences repeated. I heard a psychiatrist say to a group of theological students that many people would go to doctors rather than to ministers with their problems because medical ethics demanded sancitity of confidence. 'The physician's business is to listen,' he said, 'and the preacher's is to talk. A doctor true to his professional training never betrays his patients; never with anyone will he discuss a case. But soon or late, with the average preacher, such cases make wonderful homiletic material and they are likely to be used as illustrations.' " [20]

Should the ethics of the physician be higher than that of the clergy? Somehow the people must be led to regain their confidence that any confession made to a minister is inviolable, that it will not be betrayed by word, look, or action of any kind. The only way such can be restored is that their minister never, in private conversation or in public address, implies or states openly any confidence related to him. And yet with adequate safeguards protecting the integrity of his people a minister can garner from his daily associations with them a vast amount of material which when sifted will be of inestimable help through his sermons.

Here is a result of pastoral work which is given by Dr. Roy L. Smith to his congregation without the slightest hesitancy or apology and with great value to them. "I had been much impressed by the astonishing spiritual growth which a certain new convert was making, and wondering much at the miracle. Calling at the man's office one day to keep a luncheon appointment, I was invited to be seated in a small private room. 'I wanted to have you here just at this time,' said the business man, 'for I wanted you to share with me the finest fifteen minutes I have during the entire day.' With that he drew from out a drawer in his desk a little New Testament and pointed to a date written on the flyleaf and continued: 'That is the date of my conversion. Every day since that day I have come into this little private office, shut myself away from all business, and spent a quarter of an hour renewing the experiences of my conversion. I have found that these fifteen minutes redeem all the rest of the day for me.' " [21]

Dr. Ralph Sockman in a memorable sermon, "The Divine at the Door," pictures this symbolic scene:

"Consider the situation of the home. A young husband and wife bind themselves together to build a home. They are strong, capable, self-sufficient. A good income guarantees their union against the inroads of want. They love each other, and are loyal to each other, but they will indulge in no sentimental talk about the sanctity of marriage vows or the necessity of vicarious sacrifice. They are going to be under no illusions about this matter of love. It is a natural human thing, an attraction physical and mental. It is normal to desire children and they will rear a family. They have money to give the children excellent schooling, healthy bodies, good times. Nothing else seems to be needed. The family circle seems a completed whole. The doors are shut against the intrusions of religion. Religion does not appear necessary. Moreover it seems to cast a kind of chilling shadow over normal activities. So this family will have none of it. No gloomy shadows, no pious repressions for them.

"But how long can that family, or any other, keep its doors closed against the entrance of arresting ideas about vicarious suffering or a higher life, about the ultimate meanings and ends of living?" [22]

Did Dr. Sockman create this parable, or was there some family which he had visited that unconsciously gave it to him? It is evident that it came from living experience, and yet no one could feel he was speaking what he knew of him! Yet anyone facing such a situation would know he was speaking TO him.

THE ASSEMBLED CONGREGATION

There are occasions when in the midst of the sermon a face among the hearers will call to mind some incident, event, or thought which would slip neatly into that moment as a hand into a glove. With lightning rapidity the speaker must determine whether that illustration should be given literally, or be used with such necessary alterations as will avoid any listener's embarrassment. To the alert preacher such opportunities are not infrequent.

There are impressions and responses as well, difficult to define, but real nevertheless, which come from the congregation as they think and feel with the preacher. Experience will enable one to pick up these sympathetic messages and interpret them through the remainder of the sermon. You will do well to watch for them.

"It is said that Dr. Parker, of the City Temple, had on one occasion just given out his text, 'Unspeakable—Unsearchable,' when a vivid flash of lightning and burst of thunder startled his congregation. 'What was that?' dramatically exclaimed the preacher; and in a fashion, the masterliness of which those who have heard him will readily imagine, he linked up the sudden flash and peal with the topic of his sermon." [23]   Physical and visible occurrences such as this may not pass unnoticed to the watchful eye of him who would interpret natural events in terms of the spiritual.   I once heard a minister, perhaps not such a master as Dr. Parker, but yet a man of more than ordinary effectiveness, preach the closing sermon of a revival on the text, "The harvest is past . . .' and noticing through the open door a brown leaf falling, soon to be covered by the winter snows, he quickly called it to the congregation's attention and used it as the interest point in his appeal.   Simple as it was, the symbol was immediately convincing.

Apt and forceful illustrations from everyday life are everywhere about the preacher.   All he needs is power to see. Their particular value lies in the fact that they are so familiar that they do not attract attention to themselves.

TRAVEL

Fortunate is the minister who can travel into new and interesting places and among people of different states, nationalities, and customs.   Nature's grandeurs, the wild veery's call above the marsh, the blast-furnace stoker with muscles of steel, the Southern negroes singing in the cotton field, a conference with a statesman of a foreign country, the conversation of a Chinese coolie—all these and many others can pay tribute to the sermon. Attendance upon associations, conventions, synods, conferences, and at congresses, clubs, societies of one's brethren and of those of other persuasions, not only broaden the outlook upon life but also enhance the preacher's repertoire of materials.

It is fine if one can visit the Holy Land, Paris, or even Chicago; if one can see with his own eyes the Swiss Alps, or the surpassing beauty of the Grand Canyon of Arizona; but in these days it is not altogether necessary to travel.

Kant never was more than forty miles from his home. He was so regular in his habits in the little orb in which he moved that the natives of his village used to set their timepieces by his daily walk. Of course Kant was no painter of pictures, verbal or otherwise, but he was faithful to his task of encompassing man's thought, blazing new highways of thinking.

A minister need never wander outside his own county, although I wonder who hasn't, and still be a world traveler. He may go from the bottom of the ocean with Harold Begbie to the summit of Mount Everest, from equatorial Africa to Little America and the South Pole, from the barren Gobi desert and mountain fastnesses of high Tibet to the most populated sections of a congested metropolis, from the mass atheism of Russia to the fervent prayer of a little mother— one may, wherever he is, travel in his own reading and thinking through books and magazines to the farthest corners of

116

the earth. Fortunate is the minister who can interpret that which he sees into the warp and woof of the Kingdom of God. Many there are in these days of frequent travel who see, but few understand.

THE LAND AND THE PEOPLE

One of the most engrossing studies of our times has been that pursued by some men who have tried to determine the effect of geography upon the lives of men and nations. Such a study of Biblical lands is most rewarding.

The Plain of Esdraelon, sometimes called the "battle-ground of the centuries," severs Palestine halfway from north to south. In a very vital sense the history of the people of this little land circulates about this valley. It is the meeting place and the best fighting ground between the Nile and the Euphrates. Civilizations have fought back and forth across its level soil for ages, fertilizing the ground with human blood. Famous names, like ghosts of the past, return from its dust: Barak and Deborah, Gideon, Saul and the Philistines, "the marches and countermarches of Syrians, Egyptians, and Jews in the Hasmonean days—the elephants and engines of Antiochus, the litters of Cleopatra and her ladies," the Romans, the early Christian pilgrims, the Moslems, Napoleon, and one of the great battles of the World War. Upon a hillside near Nazareth the boy Jesus looked down into the flat valley and watched the caravans of travelers, the Roman soldiers, the pearl merchant, the peasants, journey along this highway of the world's travel.

117

How this geographical layout of hills and plain affects the entire life of the Hebrew peoples! And how valuable the knowledge of it is to the preacher who would make real to his people the life of that ancient day.[24]

A particular physical feature of the earth near Jerusalem is used by Dr. Burris Jenkins in the introduction to a sermon, "The First Easter." "Outside the present walls of the city of Jerusalem rises a rounded hill called Gordon's Calvary. The Church of the Holy Sepulcher inside the walls is built over the traditional site of Calvary and the tomb of Christ; but 'Chinese' Gordon, studying the Holy City and its environs with his keen, clear vision, found this other hill on the north side beyond the Damascus Gate, shaped like a skull, with two caverns like empty eye-sockets staring toward the city. Of course, those caves may or may not have been there for two thousand years, but certainly the present appearance of that hill tallies exactly with the description of Golgotha, the place of a skull. At the foot of the cliff, on the cityward side, there is a tomb, undoubtedly two thousand years old, hewn in the solid rock, with a great stone, flat and round like a millstone, six feet across, which rolls in a grove to cover the mouth of the tomb. It was in just such a sepulcher, and I think most probably in this very sepulcher, that the Lord lay." [25]

One who can twirl the ball of the earth beneath his gaze as Van Loon and see the effect of the land upon the people will come to a deeper understanding of life currents and not be without occasional material for use in his sermons. There is a close affinity between geography and peace! And again, whether one agrees or not, he must pause before Van Loon's statement that because of geographical factors England is becoming just an island off the Dutch coast!

THE MAGICIAN—SCIENCE

There is probably no illustration so acceptable, so sacrosanct, to a modern congregation as one from the field of science. Science has to many a modern assumed the place of authority once occupied by religion. And even to those who do not fully accept this realm of knowledge as the new messiah, there are few who do not regard it as a revealer of truth. Curiosity to know more of its mysteries makes the field attractive to the average layman. "The preacher who refuses to make himself acquainted with the main results of modern scientific research cuts himself off from the currents of present-day thought, and while he may speak to generations dead and gone he has no message for the people of his own day." [26]

Because of the mind of today and its interests, illustrations from science are apt and valuable to the sermon. It is not necessary for a minister to be a specialist in biology or physics or geology in order to use illustrations from them. An understanding of the method and viewpoint of the scientist, the major achievements and the primary values of science, is enough. From there he may range as his own inclinations direct him. A bird's-eye view of the field may be gained by reading Thomson's "Outline of Science," and books by Jeans, Eddington, and Alexis Carrel.

An analogy from science or the story of devotion of a particular man of science will not fail to be appreciated by present-day audiences.

Dr. Frederick B. Fisher is preaching on the subject, "Is There a God?" as follows: "J. Arthur Thomson, gifted, knighted, keen-spirited British scientist, who has written so abundantly and so accurately upon the history and significance of modern science, comes forward with a bit of emotion and imagery in speaking of divinity in creation. He recalls Charles Kingsley's descriptive story entitled 'Water Babies.' Arthur Thomson's scientific friends wonder a little and lift their eyes as he turns to Kingsley's imagery of Mother Nature, old Dame Nature, pictured as a rather heavy-set mother. She sits at the edge of a little pond, arms folded, serene, leisurely, indifferent as to what is happening about her. And then to the inquiry as to how she operates nature, she smiles slightly and makes reply, 'You see, I make things make themselves.' This parable pictures for Professor Thomson the energizing spirit, the living principle within all matter, generative, expansive, cohesive, expressive. A divinely living principle down underneath and within the world making things make themselves! Is not this spirit God? . . . It is but a parable of that larger inherent and instinctive law of life, which also generates changes in stones and in stars and in flowers. It leaps through wires and across the air; it pulses through history; it abides though it passes; it lives though it dies. God is inherent in life. How gloriously present at every step of the way." [27]

Certain warnings should be issued on several points.

The first is the pedantry of scientific illustration. Many a preacher so clutters up his message with such paraphernalia week after week that the people cringe when he draws forth another Frankenstein.

A second warning is that scientific facts which need of themselves to be explained make poor illustrations. An illustration should throw light upon and not make obscure.

The third warning is of the opposite nature. The preacher must be positive that whatever material or illustration he uses from any source whatsoever is not contrary to science. In no more rapid manner may he put the question mark upon his message than by relating any event or incident which is unscientific. Fact! Fact! This generation wants nothing that is foreign to truth.

GATHERING MATERIALS: LITERATURE AS A SOURCE

WHEN one steps over into the realm of literature, one enters a country so wide and of such infinite attractiveness that we may suggest in such a brief space as is allowed here only a few of the major contours. What a minister may appropriate from the writings of others will depend in large measure upon his own inclinations and upon what he feels he must know of the best literature. He may plow deeply through the classics or he may wander pleasantly through the latest fiction; wherever he goes, he will find illumination for life, some of more value than others.

LIFE'S INTIMACIES

There are men and women who have laid their souls bare to the world in their writings. From them the preacher may see and interpret similar experiences of his people. They are the persons who write of themselves, of their own lives, of their own circumstances.

There are available personal letters which reveal the intimacies of life without restraint, written that a man may tell to friends what he never expects the world to know. He writes casually or intently with self-revelation; and then some day these letters which he presumed had been burned or had found their way into the wastebasket are collected, and behold, his soul, his innermost thoughts, become common property.

It may be that among the letters of a genius or man of note an illustration may be found which will fit to perfection in your sermon. Or again it may be in the simple but penetrating letters of a noble youth, "Larry," that you may discover the very insight into the present-day young person's outlook on moral problems, such as the following:

"Some people say, 'Whose business is it how I live? I can do as I please.' Which leads me to believe that the greatest need in the world today (with the exception of a spirit of love), especially in our own country, is Responsibility. I have always felt that my body, my mind, and my soul were given to me to use for the betterment of my associates, my community, my nation; that I am the trustee of a Personality, and that I must regard it as a sacred trust. How else can I explain my presence here? I must be helpful, 'else wherefore born?' " [1]

Autobiography is filled with self-revelation of such a nature that the preacher-reader may profit not only in next Sunday's sermon but also in many to come. Rich ores are found in this mine. The reading of such a book as *Out of My Life and Thoughts,* by Albert Schweitzer, will refresh one's life as well as one's preaching.

Again there is the diary or journal, jotted down at the end of each daily journey, recording the events of life, or the motives that induced action, or perhaps the thoughts the day has brought. There is no greater self-revelation of any minister's life than the *Journal* of John Wesley. Perhaps no other man has so critically analyzed his own soul as has John Wesley. Especially valuable, therefore, is any diary which was written for self-consumption.

Reinhold Neibuhr's *Notebook of a Tamed Cynic* was written largely without any thought that it would ever be printed, but the reader can almost put his finger on the line where that intimate personal introspection ends and the realization that there will be an outward reading public begins. Of most value are the thoughts confessed to self alone.

Intimate essays on occasion have ideas and pictures which are valuable in sermons, and the preacher may with profit lay them to fee.

The Lives of Men

In talking with preachers about the theme under our consideration and in reading innumerable sermons, it is apparent that the written history of men and women, biography, holds large place in the reading schedule. There are three kinds of biography: that which is painted in too glowing colors, that which reveals only the somber and dark, and that which shows life in both its lights and shadows. Some biographers see their characters only through rose-colored glasses, some with Freudian glee depict only that which is pathological, and others can mingle the good and ill into that sincere and true picture which is life. There is probably no other field of literature comparable to biography in its material for sermonic illustration.

In one sermon, "The Power to See It Through," Dr. Fosdick uses to advantage the names of Elsner, Chopin, Socrates, Livingstone, Lincoln, Tchaikovsky, Beethoven— seven men in addition to many from Scripture. Does anyone think that such brief references as he here makes did not come from a full knowledge of the lives of these men, from having read their entire biographies? When asked on one occasion what type of book he read more than any others, Dr. Fosdick answered, "Biography." It gives one not alone illustrations innumerable, but a knowledge of men and their motives which is far deeper and much more important. If your sermons would be living realities, bring men alive from their biographies to walk your pulpit with you.

Dr. Merton S. Rice, one of the outstanding illustrators of the modern pulpit, calls many a man and woman forth from the past to tell from his pulpit events of their lives. "When the greatest musician, Beethoven, became stone-deaf, he learned that by clenching a stick in his teeth he could so hold it against the sounding-board of a piano as to detect faint sounds. How tragic a scene it must have been to witness this superb artist who could conceive and sense our greatest music, but who could not hear it. There is, however, something commandingly impressive to see that great master of music deaf of ears but responsive of soul." [2]

Or again in another sermon, speaking of the courage of priority, first things first; "You must bravely dismiss all the cheap suggestions of lesser things. . . . Here is the very heart of great living. It might easily be pointed out in the roll of earth's great, chosen by any distinction. Augustine, whose contrasting character as the world thinks of him, stands in the rugged victoriousness of his brave determination to cast aside all the implications and offerings that luring habits could suggest out of a stained past whose tendencies he broke. Today his name is almost a synonym for noble pure living, and he built it in triumph over trifling temptation. Galileo is another name that insists upon attention in this same triumphancy. He saw the truth, and though threatened and warned and persecuted by the fearstruck grovelers about him, and though branded as a deceiver and a heretic, and hurled into sufferings too great for mortal flesh to endure, he did at last cast them all aside and lead a whole world past every lesser liability into the bravest way of daring for all truth." [3]

In biography we have history as interpreted in the lives of individuals. A certain church school class studying the Life of Jesus were discussing the statement that Jesus came "in the fullness of time." The whole background of the New Testament indicates it. Jesus came at the focal point of history. This question then raised itself, "Was Jesus the product of his age or did he so impress himself upon his times as to direct their course?" It is evident that out of such a discussion the conclusion is inevitable that with the man of unusual talents neither he nor his age can be omitted and that man and his social situation are a part of the same pattern. It is necessary to understand both the environment and the man, the movements of history and the characters who are history.

When it comes to missionary biography or that of the churchmen, a twofold purpose may be served, to illustrate one's sermon and again to enlarge the congregation's knowledge of the achievements of Christianity and the Church. It is still true that "lives of great men all remind us . . ."

MYTHOLOGY?

If you ever knew mythology, let us hope that so far as your sermons are concerned you have forgotten it. For if there is anything people want today it is reality and not the homicidal wars of petty and outmoded gods. An occasional reference may not be without value, but continually to parade the dust-laden deities before a congregation dying for want of living breath is unpardonable. This is admittedly a prejudice of mine, which the demand for sincerity among the people has forced into my thinking. Yet I want to temper it with this bit from a sermon of Dr. Hough on "Vicarious Experience":

"It is well to avoid the plays of Euripides if you do not want your mind and heart and conscience to be searched by potent and penetrating rays of light. And sometimes these rays shine very far. Euripides can never quite avoid being a conscience for the Greek gods, and when his judgment is implicit rather than explicit it is all the more terribly final. In the play 'Hippolytus' the hero has given himself to the service of the chaste goddess Artemis. He has roused the hatred of Dionysus, and the god of wine has encompassed his ruin. As he lies dying you feel that somehow Artemis must do something for him. And as if in response to your desire the great goddess appears. But the death sweat is on the face of Hippolytus and the death rattle is beginning to be heard in his throat. Quite overwhelmed by the terrible situation, Artemis explains that no dweller on Olympus can witness the physical death of mortals and ignominiously vanishes. In the hour of the supreme need of her votary she has failed him. You think long, long thoughts as you hold the old play of Euripides in your hand. Your mind journeys far over time and space. You behold a green hill far away, outside a city wall. You see the suffering figure torn with agony upon the cross. You watch the Son of God going the whole length of vicarious experience and dying for men. Then you know why the Greek religion could not live. And you know why Christianity cannot die." [4]

If you can use some mythological reference in your sermon as capably as this, you have my respect. But if not, my predjudice still holds—forget mythology!

POETRY

"Nowhere else can the preacher get so much help in this power of painting pictures by the use of words as among the poets." [5] Probably only a small number in the average congregation will be familiar with the poets, but there is a widespread delight in poetry among people generally. A poem carefully selected and well-told will emphasize a thought as probably no other type of illustrative material. Well may we as preachers be students of the finest which the poets have given as messages of divine events. The higher poetry is next to the Bible in inspirational power.

In those rich sermons of Dr. Arthur Gossip which sometimes contain longer poetic quotations there come creeping couplets that are winsome and unusually appropriate, such as these:

> "Let us leave God alone,
> Why should I doubt He will explain in time?" [6]

> "And when it is time to go—go,
> And make as little fuss about it as you can." [7]

> "So in the streets I hear them say,
> Yet Christ walks with me every day." [8]

Wordsworth, Tennyson, and Browning among the older poets, along with Markham, Crowell, Oxenham, and Clark of the more recent, will open out vistas of insight to the people. The three best collections of poetry for use in sermons are the two volumes of *Quotable Poems*, edited by Clark and Gillespie, and *The World's Great Religious Poetry*, edited by Caroline Hill. The latter is the finer collection, but not so usable or quotable as the former two. Current magazines often carry poems which prove of value.

A poem should not be incorporated simply in order to have a poem in the sermon; it should truly and effectively illustrate the point at issue. The same criteria of judgment should apply to a poem as to any other illustration—namely, that it illuminates and does not cloud the issue.

Inasmuch as hymn collectors presume to change the wording of hymns to suit better the music and sentiment, it seems to me that the preacher has a perfect right to take whatever lines he desires from a poem, and if the substitution of an occasional word is better adapted to his use to make that change.

Out of a rather long poem, "Song of Myself," by Walt Whitman, any part of which is thought-provoking, Dr. Frederick B. Fisher chooses but three and a half lines, and then omits several between:

"For room to me stars kept aside in their own rings, . . . generations guided me,
All forces have been steadily employ'd to complete and delight me,
Now on this spot I stand with my robust soul." [9]

But those particular lines, arranged in that way, could do for his sermon what the whole or any more of the poem could not.

ESSAYS

The personal intimate essay, as well as others of more extended and pervasive outlook, may yield a valuable treasure. Often a quotation from one, lucid in style, not a crude stone of however ultimate value, but a shining polished gem of imperishable thought we may quote verbatim—if not too long. The fact that here is an idea from one of the great minds of all time sustaining the conclusion to which you have come is, as in debate, an authority which will have due weight with the congregation. "The only way to have a friend is to be one," says Emerson.

DRAMA

Life in our parish may seem dull and routine, but in the motives and action of our people lie the issues out of which comes the drama of life. Love and hate, self-forgetfulness and avaricious greed, noble purpose and foul betrayal, all these and every other hidden spring of living are inherent among the people we serve. In a great way or small those themes played upon by the playwriters are vibrant with life or submerged yearnings in our own city or village.

As Hamlet decides,

> "The play's the thing
> Wherein I'll catch the conscience of the king,"

so may we as well bring the playwright's art to focus upon the conscience of our people. Life's a drama and the highly focused and intense action of the stage can forcefully be used to illumine the sermon.

There is little question as to the validity of using a quotation or scene from the classic plays. No one would question using a quotation from Shakespeare, such as

131

> "Imperial Caesar, dead and turned to clay,
> Might stop a hole to keep the wind away."

But there is reason to be careful when a modern drama suits the case.

An illustration from one of the plays, "Music in the Air," which had a long run in New York and later, I believe, in the movies, might be most forceful in a sermon.

In that play an old Bavarian musician has attempted for years to compose a popular song which would make him famous, but all his efforts had proved in vain. While he pauses during another futile attempt, he hears outside his window a linnet singing. He listens, then his fingers return to the keys of the piano; he reproduces the linnet's sweet melody, later the song is published, and before long the world is singing the "music from the air." The old musician has become famous and his daughter at that moment seems to have made her way into happiness and love.

The old master muses in soliloquy, "If that particular linnet had not sung that song on that branch on that particular morning, all these things would never have happened."

What a capital illustration of the fact that, however hard we may try for the great moments of life, it is often in the fortuitous and unexpected combination of ordinary circumstances over which we have little control that life's greatest destinies come.

The question a preacher choosing an illustration from a

modern drama must answer certainly to his own satisfaction, if not to that of his congregation, is whether in using this material he has not at least inadvertently approved the play which in many another instance is exactly the opposite of his gospel. It is possible that he may hedge his illustration by disavowing allegiance to certain other parts in the drama. Possibly one preacher would find such an illustration unobjectionable, while another using the same theme would prefer to use some material, such as

> "Fortune brings in some boats
> That are not steer'd," [10]

or the couplet,

> "I knew not 'twas a giant hour
> That soon would pass away." [11]

Dramatists, the great ones, do see the issues of life, and many of their characters may be brought into the pulpit to give vitality to the accounts of eternal life. Dr. Frederick B. Fisher so uses them in this instance:

"Jerome K. Jerome, in his *Passing of the Third Floor Back* (a book that might properly be regarded as a modern Gospel), gives us a picture of Christ as a beautifully gracious, modern, humble, pervasive personality in an ordinary city lodginghouse, a stranger. He is placed among all sorts of people, cheap and ordinary and vulgar, criminal and deceitful, mean and selfish and wicked; with now and then a good spirit manifesting itself. Here you find Jesus as a lodger on the third floor back, a mere stranger, dressed as a tradesman; but every time he enters the lodginghouse where the old furniture smells of kerosene cleaning, and where the people are cheap in their talk, there is something about his presence that brings a hallowed influence into the room; the men and women are more careful in their vulgarity than they were before. Here is a cunning cheater, the cleverest man of the group, a man that belonged to a selfish race and a clever class in society; a cheater, right down to the core of his nature. He had been true to his type as a cunning cheater, utilizing all his inheritance of conceit and all the petty expression of his self-centered individuality. Finally, one day, he came quietly into the dinning room of the lodginghouse and looked into the face of this stranger. They had a brief conversation.

" 'You have always taken it for granted, sir, in all our conversation, that I was a fine fellow, in sympathy with fine ideals; but, sir, that is not what surprises me; it is to find—that you are right!'

"It was not only the passing of the third floor back, it was the passing of a cheater, it was the passing of a gambler with rotten instincts of selfish gain. It was the passing not only of the third floor back and of the cheater, but it was the transfiguration of life into greater purity and beauty. That is the essence, that is the genius of Christianity. Conversion of human action by appreciation; regeneration of human nature by expectation; transfiguration by magnetic purity. That is the scale we must always use to weigh the truth of the Christian religion." [12]

We might well conclude this section with the left-handed advice given by Lincoln to Stanton as recorded in John Drinkwater's *Abraham Lincoln, A Play*. In one of the crises of the nation, in which Lincoln and Stanton differ irreconcilably, Lincoln turns to his compatriot and asks, "Stanton, do you ever read Shakespeare?" "No," was the reply. To which Lincoln simply said, "I thought so." Had Stanton been familiar with the great dramatist, he would have understood life better and never so superficially taken the stand which he did.

Our sermons may become alive and vital through the wise use of the drama as illustrative material.

FICTION

In his fascinating and penetrating study of contemporary literature in America as it relates to religion and the man in the pulpit, Dr. Halford E. Luccock says:

"Organized religion can neglect the literature of its time only at its peril. To say that seems an utter commonplace, yet it is a tragedy which has often happened, and which has been by no means absent in the last fifteen years. The creative writing of any time is one of the most authentic sources of knowledge of the tempers and distempers of that time, in which religion must live and move and do whatever work of redemption it is to achieve. To neglect it is like a physician neglecting to take a patient's pulse or temperature; for literature is both. A striking expression of the unique value of fiction as source material for the understanding of an historical period is to be found in St. John Ervine's novel, *Changing Winds*. A social worker has been disparaging novels as useless to her in her work. Mr. Ervine thus describes the comments of another character:

" 'No wonder, he thought to himself, all reformers and serious people make such a mess of the social system when they despise and ignore the principal means of knowing the human spirit (i.e., literature).

" ' "That's a pity," he said aloud. "I should have thought that you'd find novels useful to you in your work. I mean, there's surely more chance of understanding the people of the eighteenth century if you read Fielding's *Tom Jones* than there is if you read Lecky's *England in the Eighteenth Century*."

" ' "Is there?" said Rachel. "Of course there is," Gilbert hurled at her from the other side of the table. "Fielding was an artist, inspired by God, but Lecky was simply a fact-peddler, inspired by the Board of Education. Why, even that dull ass, Richardson, makes you understand more about his period than Lecky does." '

"Often we hear ministers and others cry out at the low tone of literature, seemingly oblivious that their criticism is not so much of literature, which is a symptom, as of the life of a generation, which is a cause. . . . Many forget that the real answer is not that authors are degenerate and perverse, but that they are voices of their times." [13]

It is not the solemn duty of the preacher to parade the neurotic and lusting individuals of many of the novels across his pulpit, but even out of these novels of disillusion and defeat there come pictures which will enable the preacher to depict to his people the era in which they live, and the scene *out* of which they must mold new life for themselves and their world. The very contrast to the obsession of futility may come out of the ugly scenes.

"In the midst of much else in that modern parallel to the great Greek tragedy, *Mourning Becomes Electra,* there is the play of marionettes in the hands of fate, moved by hatred and lust, marked by almost entire absence of pity. It seems to convey an overtone of a sort of theological doctrine of defeat, of frustration and hopelessness. There was real pertinence in the remark of a Boston woman, after witnessing the five-hour production: 'Can't we find a nice pleasant morgue in which to spend the rest of the evening?' Certainly the dominant conception of *Mourning Becomes Electra* stands in sharp contradiction to Hebrew and Christian ideas, which stress both man's power to choose between right and wrong and the power of love and compassion." [14] Such observations as this can aptly find their way into the sermon.

And there is much in the present-day novelists' pictures of the current scene to bring hope and encouragement into the preacher's message. Not all of the characters are of ill repute, nor all of deterministic outlook upon life. Particularly at the present time voices are being raised in fiction which indicate the pendulum has swung from the more morose and morbid treatment of recent years to a finer and more wholesome outlook upon life.

For instance, in this magazine short story is found an insight well worth using:

"Annette Gode went on: 'I suppose you two think that because I've known poverty I'd be sobbing out my heart and throwing away my money on the poor. You can't tell me anything about the needy. Every one of these—*every one*—is shiftless, lazy, a squanderer. They don't know the value of a penny—they'll never know.'

" 'And what about it?' said the Big Doc.

" 'What about it?' repeated Annette Gode.

" 'Uh-huh, you're not arguing with me,' he said. 'You're right. Practically every misfortune of these people is brought on by their own shiftlessness, their own folly. And they don't change. I have no illusions about them—though my wife is apt to have. I'm no sentimentalist about the poor. I don't often quote that from these people will come the Irving Berlins, the Al Smiths, the Annete Godes.'

" 'Then why do you work for them?' she demanded.

"The Big Doc moved toward the stove and a shaft of late afternoon sunlight caught him, a shaft of sunlight softly kind as though in penitence for its tantrummy absence that day. It showed the Big Doc's hair in need of cutting, the white padding in his tie under the worn knot, the darned place in the trousers knee, which his wife had thought would never show.

" 'Because,' he said wearily, 'they are the children of the

world. When it's summer, they never know winter will come. It has always been that way—the weak hanging on to the coattails of the strong. It's the penalty the strong must pay. It's the thing that lifts humanity above the survival-of-the-fittest of animal life.' " [15]

There are words here that would haunt one's memory forever—"They are the children of the world. When it's summer, they never know winter will come." From a recognition of this grew the compassion of Jesus, and all the mercy ever shown by the strong for the weak.

Through fictional literature, both the novel and short story, the preacher may come to understand his times and find characters, intense situations, penetrating thoughts, to illustrate vividly his sermons. He will find it valuable to know the worst as well as the best of this literature. And of course the great fictional literature of preceding generations will provide for him insights into human character which are the same yesterday, today, and next Sunday. Never will character be delineated better than by Victor Hugo, Dickens, Thackeray. A Dr. Jekyll and Mr. Hyde walks the streets past one's church, bargains over the store counters, and sits in one's pews. Yes, many of them.

The sources from which one would choose his illustrations are infinitely varied. The accepted classics of fiction, the modern novel and short story, the fictional writings in the current magazines, all provide a rich mine from which to dig the ore of illumination.

Book Sermons

We should mention book sermons in which the preacher takes a book, either of fiction or more serious material, and uses it as the basis of the message. Dr. Stidger has outlined and illustrated this method in several of his books.[16] When a preacher takes a title such as *Magnificent Obsession,* by Lloyd Douglas, or *The Great Hunger,* by Johann Bojer, connects it closely with a great theme of the Bible, and preaches realistically to the fundamental needs of his people, there is untold value. But when a preacher merely reviews a modern book, however interestingly, without touching upon vital Christian experience, what is he more than a huckster of fiction? The advice of the late Dr. S. Parkes Cadman, who preached so truly to the hearts of men, is valid when he says, "We should contemplate human nature, not in the still and precise ways which conventional sermons adopt, but as a great novelist sees and tries to describe it." [17]

Stories

There are some preachers who hesitate to use the story-method in preaching, for they feel it is not dignified enough for the presentation of divine truth. Jesus did not look upon it in this way; in fact, he took the reverse position, that people rarely perceive truth except through story and analogy. In following the Master we have the great example for the use of stories. And in our time there are innumerable and infinitely varied stories for our use.

140

They range all the way from the fancied tale for a child, which is often deep with meaning for life, on through tales of adventure, heroic struggle, pioneering scientific research, devoted self-forgetfulness, missionary endeavor, patient endurance; and on the other hand those of defeat, self-destruction, evil consequences for family, an entire group or nation.

A preacher may epitomize the plot of a book, paint the graphic scene from an epic, or tell a simple short story.

The sources are infinitely varied. Biography, church history, history in general, novels, short stories, and books given particularly to stories will provide materials of this sort. The preacher will often hear stories. He must be positive that the facts of such related incidents are true before he repeats them. There are some compilations which have value, but they need to be touched lightly for fear that too often the preacher will drag a ready-to-hand story into the sermon by the hair of its head. Care needs to be taken also that the story is either freshly told or is not of a hackneyed and trite type probably heard on former occasions by the people.

In a sermon, "Is Christianity True?" Dr. Frederick B. Fisher gives the final testimony of the validity of the Christian experience—a life in which Christ has become real:

"Witness Jenny Lind, the Christian prima donna. I never saw Jenny Lind, but I have read avidly her biography. . . . One day I read a fascinating thing about Jenny Lind's public appearances. It appealed to my mystic sense of art and spiritual wonder. Before she would sing in any concert, or in any great dramatic production, Jenny Lind always stood absolutely alone in a closed room off the stage. She was never flustered; her secretary was pushed to the door; her maid was dismissed; the costumers were excluded; and the door was locked. It was said that she would go over in the morning, before her first appearance, to discover what kind of room would be at her disposal, and whether it could be closed absolutely and locked against all visitors. She never appeared on any stage without first having bolted the door, in a sort of upper room. She would stand in the middle of the floor and lift her voice and strike a note. It was quietly done. Then she would close her lips and let that note fill the little room. At last, with closed eyes, she would say, 'Master, Master, let me ring true tonight.' That was her prayer.

"Her friends say that when she opened the door to walk out onto the stage, she had a mystical consciousness of the presence of Christ walking before her across the stage. A personal friend reports the following dramatic sentence: 'Sometimes I hesitated and could not sing on the instant, because I was waiting for that figure to bow and smile and say, "It is all right; go ahead, Jenny." ' Lady Westmoreland writes: 'When the time came for her song —I do not know what it was—my mother used to say it was the most extraordinary appearance she ever remembered. The wonderful notes came ringing out, but over and above that was the wonderful transfiguration, no other word could apply, which came over her entire face and figure, lighting them up with the whole fire and dignity of her genius. I saw a plain girl when I went in; but when she began to sing her face literally shone like that of an angel.' In Jenny Lind Christianity was true." [18]

BOOKS OF ILLUSTRATIONS

Let me call to your attention the danger of using frequently a book of illustrations. A preacher should know that many selections made therefrom have probably already been told to his congregation. And again it is to be wondered whether an anecdote taken from such a book will not even in the retelling carry a mustiness that defeats the message. The advice of an older preacher to a class in preaching is still valid: "Use such books? Yes, perhaps! but touch them lightly."

The reason that illustrations plucked from an *Enclyclopedia of Easy Quotations* almost invariably seem stale may be realized from this quotation from Dr. James Black: "If preaching is a message plus personality, the personality should have its full and natural share. What distinguishes any two preachers? Roughly speaking, if they take a common subject, most men of similar intelligence and training say largely the same things, and deal with the same aspects of truth. The main difference lies in personality—in personal touches, in personal point of view, in personal treatment, and in personal impact. All the great preachers have been strongly individualistic." [19] Illustrations from one's own observation and experience, if vital and living, far outweigh those mummified anecdotes pulled bodily from the stock-in-trade books.

Printed Sermons

Some preachers refuse to read sermons by other ministers because they are afraid it will destroy their own originality. There is certainly plenty to be said as to the debilitating effect of preaching other men's sermons. On the other hand, how may an artist learn the highest perfection if he refuses to study the masters? A preacher needs to study the sermons of the great preachers, not to cull from them their ideas or illustrations but to see how the masters of pulpit speech treat their texts and subjects, how they handle their materials, how they drive home their arguments, and what methods they use in the art of illustration.

In such a study there will come again and again a striking illustration which will fasten itself in the reader's mind, and which he will want to note for future reference. But that too will come indirectly and not because the reader has gone as a bird of prey to feast upon the illustrative bodies found prostrate in that sermonic pasture. When in studying the sermon of another an illustration strikes fire in your imagination or kindles your heart, make it pay tribute to your sermon, and do it with a free conscience, acknowledging the source when advisable. But primarily investigate the messages of other men to learn their art, how they teach and illuminate through illustrating.

144

This should be done not only with printed sermons, for they rarely tell the spirit of the real preacher, but with sermons heard from gifted preachers. I cannot see how any preacher is not in every session of a Conference or Assembly to hear every address or sermon. We preachers have few enough opportunities to hear each other preach. Every occasion is a time to learn how it should or should not be done.

CREATING ILLUSTRATIONS

There are times when no illustration is at hand which suits the occasion. In such an instance it is possible to reconstruct from fragments an acceptable illumination or again an entirely new one may be built. This is what happens of course when a parable is created. It is not true historically in the sense that it happened in detail, but it is true in its symbolism and representation and is not impossible of occurrence.

One day I was working on a sermon, "The Silences of God." The thought of that section was the noiseless process of growth. In reading I came across an incident concerning a tree in Colorado some 400 years old. This was not quite suited to my purpose, but it gave me an idea about the giant trees of California. A look in the *Enclyclopedia Britannica* gave me my facts and this illustration: "In the redwood forest of California is a giant Sequoia tree 340 feet high and large enough at its base to encircle a house. It was an aged tree when Christ was born. It was a sturdy sapling when Moses gave the ten commandments. Its age is at least 3,000 years. How imperceptibly, how irresistibly, how noiselessly this tree grew, the silent voice of God's majesty and power." Here is a simple example of how one may create illustrations for the needed hour.

GATHERED INTO A LIVING SERMON

We may well conclude this discussion of "gathering materials" by pointing out how a minister may with artistic skill blend into a sermon illustrative material gathered both by the direct method of intense search and by the indirect method of a full life.

I heard Dr. Frank S. Hickman, of Duke University, preach at an evening service. The sermon subject was "The Wholly Other." The sermon left an indelible impression upon me, as it did upon the congregation. I did not sit there and dissect the message, for I was so compelled by its power that I was carried in thought and feeling on the conclusion. When I returned to my room, I tried to analyze his sermon from the viewpoint of illustration.

In this sermon of deep, penetrating, and compelling thought, he spoke of a personal experience of a young woman known to himself and his colleague—without violating any confidence. He pictured briefly and vividly the conceptions of God by Otto, Schleirmacher, and Barth. There were several pithy quotations with phrasing, simile, and metaphor coming out of the overflow of a creative imagination. One of these caught in my memory: "Life hangs by a slender

146

thread, and no man knows at what moment the thread may be cut."

Graphically and briefly told were several instances from Scripture. Pithily he epitomized the history of nations and peoples and from the present world situation he said. "There are faithful men of religion in Germany whose names and service will outlast Hitler's puny self-exaltation." He quoted effectively from the hymn, "Majestic Sweetness Sits Enthroned upon the Saviour's Brow." At one point he contrasted by two illustrations two ideas of God, one erroneous and the other true. The first was the contention of some that God is the projection of human ideas in a mirror and when one goes behind the mirror there is nothing. Opposed to that he gave a graphic picture of what God is and of His reality.

Occasionally there was a slight humorous twist, not a joke but enough to break the tension and elicit a smile. Then there were gestures, which are also illustrations. They were so a part of the man and the message that they were expression and power in themselves.

Here is as fine an example as I know of a preacher using variety of illustration in a single sermon, and yet with such artistry that the hearer never knew until afterwards what a wealth of material had been so skillfully brought into one compact and unified sermon. Behind all this there were two requirements of a good sermon: a Christlike conception of God, cogent for the deepest present-day thinking, and a passionate exemplification in self and his own belief.

Dr. Hickman never set out to produce this sermon to show how many types of illustration could be used in one sermon. He had a profound religious truth, God, the Wholly Other, and yet available to man. When he had finished its preparation, he probably did not realize the many different kinds of illustrations he had used. How to make real to the people this deep conviction of truth was his problem. Out of the richness of a life filled with these various materials he drew, as demands pressed upon him, those symbols, figures, and incidents which he most needed, and behold! he had demanded tribute from this vast field.

"Go, and do thou likewise!"

For the encouragement of us all it might be well to add this word from the most perfect master of illustration in the modern pulpit, Henry Ward Beecher:

"I can say for your encouragement, that, while illustrations are as natural to me as breathing, I use fifty now to one in the earlier years of my ministry. For the first six or eight years, perhaps, they were comparatively few and far between. But I developed a tendency that was latent in me, and educated myself in that respect; and that, too, by study and practice, by hard thought, and by a great many trials, both with the pen and extemporaneously by myself, and when I was walking here and there. Whatever I have gained in that direction is largely the result of education." [20]

148

VI

KEEPING MATERIALS

RECENTLY I visited with the owner, a friend of mine, a plant manufacturing sash and doors. It was not a large factory producing great quantities of run-of-the-mill stock, but rather a small institution specializing in made-to-order doors, moldings, and windows. While it had stock sizes it, like the preacher who must find illustrations for definite points in his sermons, was making products to suit particular requirements in certain specific houses.

The most interesting feature observed was the system and regularity with which everything found its exact place. There were storerooms for the standard sizes, and then the material for constructing the custom-built doors and windows was arranged so as to be easiest of access.

Lumber was piled row upon row, according to kind, quality, size. Glass in varying thicknesses and most-needed dimensions was placed easy to hand. Strips of wood were piled near a machine which, by special arrangement, could make molding of any shape and design. Paint, putty, nails, each had its specific place, so that in the shortest amount of time and with the least wasted effort the design of a certain window or door could be most effectively made. Even in this plant, where novelty was the specialty, everything could be found in its place, systematically arranged.

Every preacher wishes, and then wishes again and again, that he might be able to arrange his sermonic materials in such systematic order that, with the least amount of wasted effort and in the shortest time, he could lay his hand upon the so-much-wanted illustration. But, alas and alack, mental processes are not so easily regimented.

While illustrations are constructed out of real materials, words, similes, elements of interest and appeal, they are illusive and difficult to recall. If the preacher could bring to hand all the material, all the incidents and stories he had seen and read, he never would be in want in any sermon. It is just this inability to have what you wish when you need it that is the bane of many a preacher.

The Necessity of a Method

It is immediately apparent to anyone entering the ministry that he must decide upon some method of keeping his materials, for most of the best illustrations are fleeting.

"How pointed that is," we say. And if it is not immediately jotted down, within the day, or perhaps in five minutes, it has slipped away and, like so many opportunities, returns no more.

Illustration is the master of the preacher's destiny. If

not seized and imprisoned in some system, it mockingly chides the preacher—

> "But those who doubt or hesitate,
> Condemned to failure, penury, and woe,
> Seek me in vain and uselessly implore—
> I answer not, and I return no more!" [1]

The strange thing about a system to retain the fleeting illustrations is that it too is always puzzling, uncertain, and rarely satisfactory. Some system the preacher must have, only to realize in his greatest hour of need that it does not always work!

If the preacher could have his materials readily at hand, as in the plant I visited, much of the agony of soul in the hour of sermon preparation would be saved. Often when a particular sermonic illumination is needed, he must rush distractedly through his mental storehouse, searching in hidden corners and behind piled-up and useless litter trying to find some clue to his enigma.

THE PERFECT SYSTEM

I had hoped in this discussion to present the perfect method by which the preacher would be able to have always at hand the most valuable illustrations. I do not possess such a system. Nor have I through reading of other preachers' methods of sermon preparation or by talking with preachers who are masters in this field been able to discover the ideal and unimpeachable plan.

151

The reason for this should be apparent. We are not builders with physical blocks, but artists of the soul. There are categories and principles which must be observed as in any art, but they are not mechanical and are not subject to the same classification as lumber, glass, and paint.

Here is the advice from experience of an artist in sermon illustration, Dr. James Black: "Don't be hectored into believing that you ought to adopt those artificial docketing methods that suit a business man or a railway ticket office— schedules, systems, fancy drawers with tickets on wires. Personally, that type of thing would wring me as dry as a sucked orange. But nevertheless, have the distinct methods that suit yourself and your work, and then honor them. You can have any methods you like so long as you have methods." [2]

No more memorable advice comes from this great preacher than these words. That he has method is evidenced from the reading of any of his books or sermons. And yet he says of himself, "I know that my own methods, my desk for instance, would scare many a prim precisian, but nevertheless, I have the order that seems to suit me." [3]

So instead of trying to give you the perfect system, which never was and never shall be, I hope to point out from the writings and conversation of preachers about their own preparation methods, and from my own experience and observation, certain suggestions out of which you may build your own methods, or improve those you now use.

KEEPING MATERIALS

Approaching the Ideal

Once I asked Dr. George Buttrick, whose picturesque style as well as vivid illustrations are unique, how he kept his materials. He gave this surprising answer: "I am fortunate enough to possess a photographic memory. Once having seen anything in print, I can usually recall it verbatim. Even months afterwards I can see again an incident I have read and its location on the page. For instance, in writing a book on one occasion I quoted a couplet which it was impossible for me or the publishers to locate to determine the source for copyright privileges. We searched diligently. Finally it was discovered as only two lines from a larger poem which I had read only once more than a year previously."

Some men's minds are built on that order. If so, they have God to thank for the gift. And if you have that kind of memory, you would do well to skip to the next chapter. But, as most ministers do not preach in gothic cathedrals, neither are their minds of that architecture. Yet it is just as necessary for the little frame church on the hill to have windows as it is for the great temple. It is as imperative for the preacher with a fallible memory to have illustrations as it is for his more fortunately gifted brother. If we cannot hang illustrations with regularity in the halls of memory, it is necessary for us to find some other method of keeping them—for in the moment of last resort, we must produce them.

In a conversation or in reading a book the preacher comes

upon an illustration that he feels is worth preserving. He does not need it for next Sunday's sermon, but it illustrates a religious truth upon which he may preach some day. His memory may not be trustworthy, and this illustration is worth keeping. How shall he proceed to store it for the future?

BOOK-MARKING

If the incident is found in a personally owned book, it may be marked and then, on a blank page in the back, a note of reference may be recorded. When the book is finished, there may be just a few notes; but probably there will be a page or two of them, with page numbers of the various matters noted. These references will thus provide an index of the usable materials in the book. There are many men who use this method. Dr. O. S. W. McCall says: "I mark the books that I read so that I may find again what I want should my memory indicate to me that what I want is somewhere in the book." [4] It is advisable to review these references occasionally so that they may be remembered.

A minister who keeps his magazines on file may wish to do the same with them by marking the incidents and noting the references on the margins of the last page or two. A friend of mine recently purchased two back copies of the *Reader's Digest* which completed his file of this publication. Practice in this method of marking will yield increasing results. Books and magazines thus become associate ministers.

Notebooks

If the illustration is found in a library book or one borrowed from a friend, how may it be preserved? Most ministers, like Phillips Brooks, keep a notebook in which they record a suggestion or a more elaborate outline of the incident. This notebook should also contain illustrations that are found outside of books, arising from pastoral visiting, travel, nature, and the imagination. There are many kinds of notebooks, but each preacher should choose the one best fitted to his personal use.

Dr. S. M. Berry, of the Congregational Union of England and Wales, says: "I would not have you think that I depended entirely upon the inspiration of the moment or of the week. I had a sort of jumbled-up commonplace book in which I put suggestions of all kinds, and generally with a sermon in view. It was a book I carried about with me so that any vivid point of conversation, any thought which leapt up from the pages of a book, was at once jotted down." [5]

Dr. Raphael H. Miller, pastor of the National Christian Church, Washington, D. C., "is an inveterate keeper of notebooks, in which he jots down texts, subjects, and suggestions for sermons. He has accumulated a small library of these little books, indexed ready for use." [6] "Ordinarily I read and read to the saturation point by way of first preparation," states Rev. James M. Gillie, of the Paulist Fathers, New York. "As I read I make notes. If the jotting down of a note starts my mind a-going, as it almost always does, I write swiftly, staccato style, no sentences, in the scratchiest way." [7]

There are two questions one needs to answer in regard to his notebook. First, is it convenient to carry with me wherever I go? Some of the finest illustrations come from the most unlikely places and at the most inopportune times for listing them. Unless recorded they fade from memory. A preacher cannot go about carrying a bulky and ungainly notebook. A small pocket-size book is necessary. Second, is the material so arranged as to be immediately available when preparing the sermon? There are preachers who have splendid notebooks piled on a shelf and covered with dust. There is much valuable material in them, but it is uninviting for use. Some method must be used for keeping this material up-to-date and having it available when needed. The test of a notebook, like a good servant, is not only its dependability but also its availability. It should be handy both for recording the illustration and for using it.

An Index System

In preference to a bound notebook, many ministers use cards or small sheets of paper. These cards are of practical size, usually fitting the pocket. Some of them are postal card size, $5\frac{1}{2}$x$3\frac{1}{4}$ inches. A better size is $5\frac{3}{4}$x$3\frac{3}{4}$, just enough larger for a typewriter and to contain more writing, but not too large to fit easily into one's pocket. A printer will cut out 500 of these from bond paper for a few cents. Paper is cheaper than cards and more easily handled.

Whether one uses cards or paper, one can build "an ever-growing and ever-dissolving notebook."

Some men keep these cards or paper slips in an indexed file. "As to my method of sermon preparation," states Dr. William Stidger, "I get an idea and file it away in a carefully kept filing system. That idea gathers material like a snowball." [8]

The most complete system of which I know is that of Bishop George Craig Stewart. Let him tell how he uses it in sermon preparation: "I make a rough brief outline to secure sound structural treatment. The second stage is to take that outline and elaborate it. In doing this I utilize the index system which for nearly thirty years I have developed. Every book as it is read, and this means several books a week, bears upon its last page or two a topical index created as I go along. When the book is read my secretary indexes these topics on cards which now number a great many thousands. All magazines are read and marked for clipping and filing. When, therefore, I come to the elaboration of my outline, such books and clippings as may be involved in the subjects which develop in the outline are carefully searched for allusive and illustrative materials." [9] A minister can build such a system without a secretary.

The card system can be used without indexing. As the cards accumulate, they can be kept in stacks which are held together by rubber bands. In the upper left-hand or upper right-hand corner a key word can be placed to indicate the content of the illustration. If the minister will go quickly

157

through the stacks once every month or two, he will become so familiar with the contents that he can easily locate any illustration which they contain. In going through the file or stack, those illustrations which have become outgrown or out-of-date can be removed and thrown away. In this manner the file can be kept up to date.

THE USE OF ENVELOPES

Some ministers use a system in which they have a large number of envelopes, marked for different subjects. Into these they place materials and illustrations upon particular subjects. Stephen S. Wise of New York City, one of the world's outstanding rabbis, tells of his method of preparation as follows: "As for preparing a sermon and speech, I have twenty to thirty and perhaps even more envelopes on my desk containing material on things about which some day I am going to preach. As I read and think, I make memoranda and put the items into different envelopes. A great deal of this material I shall never use, but again it is a case of a sermon ripening rather than being delivered and prepared *ad hoc* or delivered impromptu, save for a few days' preparation." [10]

CLIPPINGS

Most preachers find difficulty with newspaper and magazine clippings. If they are marked in the magazine or pamphlet, they are hard to find. If they are cut out, they are difficult to preserve. Three solutions seem possible, each usable, but none entirely satisfactory. The first is the use of labeled envelopes into which the clippings are placed. The envelopes are marked by general classifications, such as "prayer," "co-operation," "the church," etc. The second is the use of a scrapbook, into which the clippings are pasted. Like the bound notebook, such material is not always easily available. Yet such a book or series of books has advantages. Again, a file of clippings can be built up using uniformly large sheets of thin cardboard of some size up to 13x11 inches. These are indexed and the materials from newspapers and magazines are pasted on the appropriate sheets. This latter method makes it easier both to file the clippings and to locate them when desired.

Establishing a System

A number of different methods of keeping the illustrations have been indicated. Of course no preacher would attempt to use all, or even a majority, of them. Yet he will need to settle upon some method which will constitute a way satisfactory to him. The kind of notebook he will use should not depend on the convenience of the moment, but upon the work he anticipates accomplishing during a lifetime in the ministry. Keeping illustrations for future use takes time and work, but it should be done with the least loss of time and with a view to easy availability in the actual preparation of the sermon. Whatever the system, it should be as compact as possible. Some men are hampered with a too-exacting system; others cannot produce their best without an extensive procedure.

A minister can be certain that if he follows some method of accumulating his illustrations, having on hand always far more than he will ever use, his preaching will be much more illuminating and helpful to his people. Dr. Raymond Calkins says: "The preacher is constantly collecting materials bearing on the sermons which he proposes to preach. This gradual accumulation gives a sermon a certain richness and fullness when preached, which it cannot possess if it is got up between Sundays." [11]

What might be a good method of preservation for one man would be killing routine for another. What would be satisfactory notes and records for one preacher would be woefully inadequate and far too brief for someone else. Practically any preacher can find a method which is satisfactory for his purposes. Many of us could improve the method we now use by intelligent and painstaking effort. And our sermons thereby would be enriched and improved.

RELAXATION

Some of the best illustrations are not kept in files. They never can be cornered ahead of time. They are buried somewhere in past experience, when it was never anticipated that they would be good illustrations. Yet, if the preacher could only recall that conversation or that incident in a book he once read, it would be profitable to the sermon now being prepared. An impression made upon the mind, so the psychologists say, is there forever. It is never lost. Dropped down into the subconscious, it lies there sleeping; but it would be vital to this sermon if only it could be awakened. Fortunately this can be done often.

Let us suppose that this is a diagram of our mental state, The point "A" is the peak of consciousness. "B" is the subconscious. The small space above the dotted line contains all the conscious thought now available. That which is below, immense in any person, contains all the experiences one has ever had in life. Consciousness is little more than a point above the subconscious. If by any means the preacher could lower this level, represented by the dotted line, so that it would include material not usually available, he might secure illustrations and ideas which would materially assist him in the sermon.

This can be achieved by a period of relaxation and meditation. If by intense thinking on a subject the attention can be focused to the smallest point, and then, with the theme still in mind, by relaxation lower the level so that his thought sinks deeper into the less conscious, often material becomes available which never would be found otherwise.

For instance, intense thinking focuses the mind on the subject, narrowing the conscious thought to nearly a point, thus, Then, by physical and mental relaxation, dropping off almost into sleep, yet refraining from sleep, the conscious level is suddenly but gently lowered, thus Associations built up in the time of intense thinking will reach down into the subconscious. Meditative reflection will follow these leads into mind experiences, incidents, events, stories, sometimes long-forgotten, often never intended as a part of a sermon, but which now are most useful for it. Immediately after they are seized they should be written down, or else they will quickly slip back into the subconscious.

If a preacher, after careful preparation, searching for the truth, prayer, and hard work on his manuscript, will then relax and let his thoughts go where they will, often ideas and illustrations will come forward to assist him. Sometimes nothing happens. At other times the best illustrations, which have been hidden in the subconscious, will become available. The Spirit of the Lord labors with us in the intense search for the most suitable illustrations to lead His people; He also leads into pleasant pastures and beside still waters when we have entrusted ourselves in meditation to His leadership.

BUILDING ILLUSTRATIONS INTO SERMONS

AN architect planning a beautiful house, as a musician who composes a symphony, is motivated by his own initiative, ingenuity, and originality. His greatness in his profession is largely dependent upon his own particular genius.

And yet the home or the symphony must be planned in conformity to fixed rules of composition observed by all architects, composers, and artists. The physical and mental attributes of the individual artist, such as the hearing of the musician, the eyesight of the painter, or the vision of the preacher, affect his facility according to their degree of excellence. But, added to this individual apperception, there must be a technique which can be achieved through study. This observance of the principles of the art is as essential as the gift of prophecy itself.

The great preachers of the ages from the early prophets to the present hour, although often unlettered men, observed the basic principles underlying preaching and sermonic illustration. Often out of sheer necessity there was forced upon the proclaimer of divine truth the illustration which was imperative in that moment.

There are principles which apply to all art, and preaching is no less an art than sculpture or dramatics. Although varying in infinite application with individual artists, there are four principles which have been developed in the arts which must be observed. All art has movement, rhythm, unity, and perspective. These are regulative principles, the fundamentals of which are inviolable. Liberty in originality, as in government and morals, is not license, but playing the game within the rules. In the same way there are fundamental principles of sermonic illustration, the violation of which leaves the hearers unimpressed, vague in mind, perhaps repugnant toward the illustration or truth presented.

It is not easy to fix or describe the rules of sermonic illustration because they are affected by each social situation, each different community, each individual congregation, and the preacher's own disposition. This chapter is not an attempt rigidly to outline certain rules, but rather to suggest underlying principles and technique valuable in building the illustrative material into forceful sermons. Their observance will not bind the preacher within narrow confines, but will enable him to enlarge his powers and preach more effectively.

LOCATION OF ILLUSTRATIONS

Let us turn first to the places in the sermon where illustrations may be used. It is possible to use an illustration in the introduction, at each major point, perchance for a minor topic, as a transition from one thought to another, and again at the conclusion. It is exceedingly doubtful if a preacher should have all these windows in one house, but such are the possibilities.

THE INTRODUCTION

Since the introduction has as its purpose the opening of the subject, the raising of a question, the awakening of interest, or the creation of a sympathetic atmosphere, it is often advantageous to start with an illustration. It may be an incident, a personal experience, a current event, or two figures placed in contrast.

With the possible exception of a pointed and living question thrust upon the congregation, there is no means of gaining attention and developing interest better than by simile, incident, or story.

In the following example Dr. Charles F. Wishart gains attention immediately, creates an atmosphere for the sermon, and leaves a lasting picture to haunt the imagination. The title of the sermon is "Facing the Sea."

"Whereunto shall I liken this generation? Perhaps the picture may be brought before you by the parable of Atlantic City. It is, as you know, the world's playground. It is a place of vast crowds, varied amusements, much noise, the 'big parade' of wealth and luxury, of jazz music and the latest dances; at its worst a place of some vulgarity, and at its best a melee of jostling contacts with all sorts and conditions of men.

"Yet, not because of these things, but in spite of them I love to go there. For it is the easiest and most convenient way to catch the sight and the smell and the glorious music of the sea. I love that rolling expanse of majesty and constantly changing beauty. I love it in all of its moods.

"But the tragedy of Atlantic City is that so few really attend upon the sea. Thousands crowd the amusement places. Other thousands haunt the auction shops. People sit all day long, not to listen to the infinite voices from that majestic expanse of ocean, but gaze at the Boardwalk and its hurrying, overdressed crowd, its people in overdone costumes and its hotels in overdone architecture. They listen to the noise of its radios and jazz bands. Some even welcome the noise and dash and clatter to drown the voices of the sea. For sometimes that sea speaks in tones deep and solemn and challenging, and there are those who fear to hear it. But even so, on every pier there are a few seats, the farthest out, which face toward the sea. On these front seats you may see men and women, sometimes little children, at far-off gaze, drinking in the wonder and the majesty of the mighty ocean. And at night, when the hurrying feet are at last stilled upon the Boardwalk, and the traffic and din die down, through the open windows there come the steady surf beat, the fresh exhilaration of the winds which blow from far-off shores, the mystic breath of the tides.

166

"So is this generation in its attitude toward the future life.

"Men are faced toward the noisy and garish Boardwalk, and they are not contemplating the eternal sea. . . . But all the while there have been men and women—far more than we realize—who, in the midst of the din and hurly-burly, have chosen their seats so they could calmly sit out and look over that eternal sea." [1]

One word of warning needs to be given. Under almost every circumstance, except an illustration to create atmosphere or a parable, the introductory illustration should be short, the shorter and more impressionistic the better. It must be remembered that this illustration is to *introduce* the theme. It is the porch to the house, and should not be as large as the building itself.

How quickly and easily these men usher you into their sermonic homes:

"Coleridge said somewhere that Don Quixote is reason without common sense and Sancho is common sense without reason, while both are necessary to the integrity of man." [2]

"Every evening, from the top of the towering Palmolive Building just north of the Chicago Loop, the Lindbergh Light swings its long finger slowly round the dark horizon; and even the clouds in a murky sky are illuminated when that powerful beam touches them. Just so down the generations, in the Bible and out of it, great souls in whose minds and hearts the light of God has shone forth, have surveyed the horizon of mystery within which our human life is set, and with a flash of insight have lit up the obscurities that puzzle and confuse the rest of us." [3]

"That which soars high will have sparse company. Flies move in swarms, but eagles never." [4]

THE CONCLUSION

It is noteworthy that many of the best sermons of the day end with an appropriate story.

"Skyscraper Foundations," Dr. Roy L. Smith concludes with this cumulative paragraph: "All the skyscraper men of history have had this faith. Luther, standing in the presence of his persecutors, is unmoved, saying, 'Here stand I; I cannot do otherwise.' Lincoln, in the darkest moment of the Civil War, says, 'I am not concerned to know whether God is on our side; but I am determined to know that we are on God's side.' John Wesley, standing beside the bed whereon one of his humble and faithful saints lay dying, said, 'Thank God, our people die well.' Stephen, looking up into heaven, saw the Lord Christ, and died praying for his own killers." And then he summarizes briefly his thesis: " 'He that saveth his life shall lose it,' said Jesus, with a deep note of concern in his voice, for well he knew that life must be lived with abandon. With the marks of divinity upon him, man has been designed for greatness, and the redemption of Jesus is a redemption from smallness." [5]

Dr. Clovis Chappell's sermons are popular and widely read among preachers. In one of his latest books, *Sermons from the Psalms,* ten of fifteen sermons close with an illustration of more than usual worth. Practically every sermon of Dr. George W. Truett ends with an effective incident. Dr. Miles H. Krumbine, one of the youngest ministers of power, concludes every sermon in *Little Evils That Lay Waste Life* with one or more suitable and epitomizing illustrations. Dr. Harry Emerson Fosdick concludes his sermons with a question or forceful statement, but almost invariably fortified with attractive and powerful illustrations. Of the sermons in *The Power to See It Through* fifteen of twenty-one so end.

It is interesting to note that these masters of modern preaching use many different kinds of illustrations and bring them forth in a variety of forms. They run no danger of ruinous repetition of the same type of conclusion. It is fatal if the congregation, sensing the end of your sermon, say to themselves, "Now for the final story."

A study of the various preachers in this particular is most rewarding to your own preaching. Take, for instance, Dr. Fosdick's sermon, "When Life Goes All to Pieces," [6] which concludes, "The glory of everything lies in its organization. These windows are made up of bits of colored glass, but, when they are organized, how beautiful! Great music is composed of separate sounds which anyone can make, but when they are organized, how glorious! A home is made up of separate individuals, but when a great mother organizes them, how marvelous! So existence is handed to us, a mass of helter-skelter items, but life is created by personalities whose faiths and hopes and loves draw everything together and make a whole."

Contrast that with this illustration on "Family Religion": "Every summer when I go up to my Maine island I find some trees that have blown down—too many branches above ground and not enough rootage below ground. And every fall when I come back to New York I find some lives that have broken down for the same reason—too much strain, not enough staunchness; too much modern life, not enough deep religion. Some of you who are not conventionally religious, but who do care about the moral welfare of this nation, may well listen to John Ruskin on the downfall of Venice. 'The decline,' he says, 'of her political prosperity was exactly coincident with that of domestic and individual religion.' Just so! What about the church in your house?" [7]

How potent is this story concluding another sermon in a far different and even more powerful manner:

"A monument, so I am told, has been erected on the coast to the officers and crew of a wrecked vessel, who at the cost of their lives kept the high tradition of the sea. The wreck came in a dreadful storm, and despite their efforts the lifeboats were smashed and everyone was drowned. It was noted, however, that the only bodies to reach shore were those of passengers wearing life belts. Evidently there had not been enough for all and the officers and crew had gone without them so that their bodies sank and were lost. One day, it is said, a rollicking group of boys on a hike came to the monument, as merry youngsters as one could see, apparently without a serious idea in their heads, until one of them, out of boyish curiosity, asked what the monument was all about. So the leader told them of the officers and crew who tried to save others when they could not save themselves. The boys grew quieter and quieter until one of them took off his cap and then the others took off their caps too, and they stood there mute witnesses to one of the profoundest facts in human nature, that nothing in this world reaches so deep, takes hold so hard, and lifts so long as vicarious self-sacrifice.

"If we here today could be persuaded how desperately this world needs us at our best and then could be brought face to face with those great souls who have cared enough to suffer for mankind, until we stood before the cross of Christ as those boys stood before the monument, every person here would be saying two things to himself: first, I ought not to be the way I am; and second, No man need stay the way he is." [8]

Here are the conclusions of three sermons preached by the same man to the same congregation in which illustration has been used with telling force, but each in a far different manner from the other.

The conclusion of the sermon must bring the message to focus. There are times when you will want to conclude with a summarizing statement, or say to your people, "This is the conclusion to the matter." Or again you may end with a searching question. But there is no method of touching both heart and mind more effectively than by leaving a vivid picture. The illustration has a valid and useful place and the preacher planning to use one for his sermon should prepare it with much care.

Each Major Division

Usually there ought to be an illustration for each major division of the sermon. Not only should the truth be presented or argued, but also it should be seen. Many of the finest evangelistic preachers, not to say evangelists, give a brief statement of truth, and then proceed to tell a story which illustrates that truth. This is not a trick pulled out of the bag, but a fundamentally effective method of presenting the truth. It was often the means by which Jesus reached his hearers.

Certainly in each major division of the sermon there ought to be at least one illumination of more than passing notice. This need not be long, for a sharp thrust of piercing simile or phrase will reach the objective.

Dr. Arthur Gossip is ready to launch forth in a new direction in his sermon, "How Others Gained Their Courage," and does so with a concise picture that lasts through the entire division: 'Wordsworth tells us that his greatest inspirations had a way of coming to him in the night, and that he had to teach himself to write in the dark that he might not lose them. We, too, had better learn this art of writing in the dark. For it were indeed tragic to bear the pain, yet lose what it was sent to teach us." [9]

172

Good judgment will have to be used as to how much light needs to be thrown upon the truth, the kind and type of illustration most suited, and whether at this point it needs to be brief or more at length. But in each major division there is presumably place for at least one illustration.

Minor Points

There are times when minor points in the argument or thought should be illuminated. Certainly, the landing on the staircase of a residence is not as important as the second floor or the living-room, and yet it generally has its window. It is sometimes true that the major premise is fairly clear and is accepted by the congregation without dispute, but some little turn of the argument may need illumination. It is often by some little change of direction that the skillful preacher can save his congregation from tripping in the dark.

Transitions

The difficulty that faces most immature preachers is transition from one thought to another. So often young preachers, and older ones too, leave their congregations with one thought and suddenly turn to another thought without the slightest hint of the change. Every preacher recognizes the difficulty of shifting smoothly to a new idea.

Of course there are the time-honored methods, "firstly, secondly, thirdly," or such a phrase as "now we will consider further. . . ." But these are exceedingly trite. It is not only advantageous but convenient for the preacher to bridge

173

the gap with an illustration that carries the hearer naturally from one thought to another. It can be done briefly or otherwise as the situation justifies. It might be a beautifully worded sentence sensing a new direction, or a brief example, or even a longer story. The skillful handling of the change by means of a suitable illumination can, without jar or loss, direct a congregation. Illustration used in this way is not common, but it is the height of art in public speaking and brings a congregation to an unspoken sense of appreciation.

In passing from one division of the sermon, which apparently has been understood, to another division not so easy to understand, the following illustration exemplifies what can be done:

"As the clear waters of the Ohio River flow into the muddy current of the Mississippi, so the matter we have just considered, which is easily understood by all, flows into our next thought which is colored by the controversial soil of many minds and lives through which it has passed. Let us hold fast the clear truth of our first proposition, that it be not muddied or lost in the questionable elements of the second. Our first basic principle of moral conduct should add its power in the confused issue we now face." By means of this illustration the congregation is prepared for stiffer stuff and the discussion of the second proposition is made easier for both preacher and people.

We find, then, that illustrations may be used in the introduction, the conclusion, as part of each major division, to illuminate some minor obscurity, and in passing from one division to another.

WARNINGS

Several warnings should be issued as to the placing of illuminative material. Nothing is so fundamental in a sermon as maintaining a proper proportion of illustration and the other contents.

GREENHOUSES

Be sure that you do not have too many illustrations lest, instead of a symmetrical building, you construct a greenhouse. This is particularly true of the preacher whose mind naturally turns to metaphors. "Spurgeon has said concerning metaphorical illustrations: 'THEY SHOULD NOT BE TOO NUMEROUS. . . . Some men seem never to have enough of metaphors; each one of their sentences must be a flower. They compass sea and land to find a fresh piece of colored glass for their windows. . . . Flowers upon the table at a banquet are well enough; but as nobody can live on banquets, they will become objects of contempt if they are set before us in lieu of substantial viands. The difference between a little salt with your meat and being compelled to empty the salt-cellar is clear to all.' Here we have four metaphors in immediate succession to illustrate the principle of moderation in the use of metaphor—an admirable example of the violation of a principle in the very act of enforcing it." [10]

Too much accumulation of simile and metaphor defeats the purpose and confuses the people. Clean, clear-cut, forceful speech is much to be preferred. The practice of stringing stories together without much thought between them is of doubtful value. The congregation may be entertained and delighted by the fancies and incidents paraded before them, but it will not be convinced. The test of a sermon is not whether it entertains but whether it convicts.

DUNGEONS

The opposite peril awaits the preacher, that of having too few "windows" and too many "blank walls." I recently heard the same preacher on two occasions. Both sermons were packed with thought, one hopelessly dull and the other appealingly alive. In the first I was stifled in a dark pit with narrow, barred gratings; in the second I entered a house of color and beauty which was well lighted in every room. I came away from the first depressed, and left the second rejoicing over my tasks in God's world. The first sermon could have been as helpful as the second, if the preacher had given more attention to his "windows."

As between the two temptations, young preachers are most inclined to recite facts without properly and sufficiently illustrating them. I have talked with many laymen about their preachers' messages and they think that the average preacher is particularly deficient at this point. What he says is true and often well thought out, but exceedingly dull and uninteresting. It takes work, hard work, to build into one's messages enough instances to make them inspiring; but at the peril of one's ministry, this danger of too few illustrations must be avoided.

BAY WINDOWS

There was a style in windows that suited other generations, but is to a large extent passing with the modern, efficient, and more attractive home. When people had more time and room they added a bay window or so. You see such houses yet, remnants of the day when three-faced windows jutted out from the wall, and added little to beauty and less to efficiency and cleanliness. One does not get more light from such affairs, as the mullions between the sashes tend to keep out the light. Two plain windows would give more illumination.

There is also a style in sermons which prefers "bay windows" to "plain sashes." When a preacher has thirty minutes to deliver his sermon, his illustrations should be brief and compact. Avoidance of length, unnecessary phrasing, and excess description is a virtue. Illustrations which compass too much are like the bay window which obscures rather than admits light. It is surprising how much an illustration can be deleted without losing its value. Study the parables of Jesus to see the art of brevity at its best. The best short story amazes the reader by telling so much so briefly.

Illustrations which are lengthy prolong the sermon and leave nothing to the imagination. The illustrations ought to be prompt, clean, accurate, quick.

Selecting the Illustration

In the selection of an illustration certain considerations should be carefully weighed.

"Illustrate your sermons," says Dr. John A. Kern, "but do not indulge the weakness of sermonizing your illustrations." [11] It is comparatively easy, but of questionable value, to use illustrations merely to comment on them. The framework of the house should first be constructed, and then the windows added. Many sermons are like the dummies in department store windows, attractively clothed but on wooden or wax figures. "There should be in all our preaching more reading matter than pictures, a great deal more." [12]

In preparing a sermon the preacher should begin with his proposition, and develop its argument until it is conclusive. As illustrations come to him, or as he finds suitable exemplifying material, he should make notes of them to be drawn upon later as needed.

Or again he can take an idea, think it through to its logical conclusion, and then present it in the form of a striking likeness. Henry Ward Beecher once wrote out two pages of argument against the ultra-Calvinistic doctrine of Divine justice. He saw that it would be too much for the people. He struck out the whole of it and wrote instead one line: "God is not a bundle of thunderstorms." [13]

It must have taken considerable grace to have substituted one line for two pages of comprehensive thought which would have pleased his vanity in delivering. But for many preachers the reverse is true. It takes more grace to work out clearly and forcefully the thought of the sermon, refraining from preaching in a train of loosely connected anecdotes.

There is a general law that ought to be followed invariably: Never take an illustration and build a sermon around it.

Of course there are a few occasional exceptions. At certain times Jesus presented his truth in a story without comment. At rare moments the best preachers have done likewise. It might be well in this time for preachers to tell a story like Nathan to David, say, "Thou art the man," and leave it at that. The highest genius is required in such an instance and the preacher should make such a presentation with careful forethought, knowing what he intends and that it can be accomplished best in this way alone. Henry Van Dyke's *The Other Wise Man* is an illustration of such usage.

But premeditated use of illustration to carry the primary burden is a far different thing from taking a good story and developing the ideas to suit it, or to use a few ideas to bridge between many stories. The sermon is to be a thoughtful presentation of truth, reasonable, intelligent, with cases in point to give light.

THE RIGHT ILLUSTRATION

When a preacher is in the midst of his preparation there will occur to him several examples which might be used, or he may have one that almost fits the situation. It will be necessary for him to search, locate, discard, search again, never satisfied until he has the perfect illustration.

There are many Christian people who are living acceptable lives, according to prevailing standards, yet considering their abilities and training are far below the life they might be living. A minister will not be satisfied to have his sermon fairly well illustrated when he can by searching for the exact illumination have his message proclaim the highest truth as it is in Christ.

Every preacher should know well his own congregation. What will suit one group may not be effective with another. It is currently said that city people came from the country. This is one of the many half-truths. Multitudes of city-born and bred people know little or nothing about life on a farm. Many illustrations from rural life will be as valid to them as to the farmer, but many others are as alien as though they were in a foreign language. While the automobiles, newspapers, magazines, education, and the radio have brought the country people much nearer to the city, there are areas of urban life from which illustrations would darken their conception rather than enlighten it.

"The Commuter's Sermon," suggested by Dr. Halford Luccock, would mean nothing to the farmer or small-town parishioner. But it would command immediate attention from the host of present-day commuters who daily ply between city and rural home. "For the last week of his life Jesus was a commuter. Every morning he went into the city to do his work. Every evening he went back to the little quiet place in the country to spend the night. . . . Here is an aspect of Jesus' last week which comes home very closely to

180

a great army of hurrying, thronging people. The trains, the street cars, busses, and ferries bring into the cities every day millions of people whose regular movements on the shuttle of traffic are exactly those of Jesus as he journeyed back and forth from the hillside of Olivet to the crowded streets of Jerusalem." [14]

The preacher will want to select the illustrations which are most likely to meet the requirement of his particular congregation. An illustration which must be explained first is a poor one.

On the other hand in most congregations there are greatly mixed interests and appreciation, the educated and the uneducated, literary minds and newspaper minds, young progressives and older conservatives. While the preacher will not desire to lower his message to the tabloid level, yet he must be certain that everyone, in so far as he is able to make it so, comprehends the truth. He will find that one example suits one group, while another group will respond best to an illustration of a different nature. All should be helped to comprehend, and the preacher should search, discard, and search again until he has in each case found the right exemplification.

Dr. Merton S. Rice has a truth which he desires all of his congregation to understand, and he reveals it in two entirely different pictures:

"The seat of all our trouble is sin in the soul, not the surface soil of our hands. I had an Indian guide in the big north wilderness. We were sitting around a little fire one cold snow-driven night, before making our beds on the snapped-off boughs of the kindly balsams with which we had constructed a hurried lean-to, as a shelter from the storm. Another guide who sat within the ring around our fire looked at my guide, a quiet, non-talkative Indian, and said, 'Tom's hands don't show dirt.' Tom grinned silently over his Indian advantage.

"Maybe ultimately that is a human truth. For really these hands of ours do not show the dirt. The actual dirt is a much more deeply set matter. Though your hands be washed to snow whiteness, the discerning etiquette of Jesus in condemning accusation sees the seat of all the sin in the heart. Shakespeare snatched up this luminous fact, and set it in one of his famous and familiar scenes. The wretchedly guilty and spotlessly washed queen goes pacing to and fro in the relentless scourings of her unchanging guilt, as it obstinately stares at her. 'Out, damned spot! out, I say!' But the waters of all the seas could not cleanse, nor could all the perfume of Arabia sweeten that little crimson hand." [15]

"Fresh" Illustrations

I heard Dr. Ivan Lee Holt, then president of the Federal Council of Churches, deliver a sermon in which every illustration was fresh and vivid, culled from the wide world, but not a single one hackneyed. There is a need in present-day preaching for contemporary examples, for instances which are of the modern age. To meet the rigid requirements of the modern mind and current life, there must be a change in preaching, not in the fundamental content, for we preach the unsearchable and unchanging riches of Christ, but by new interpretation and new insight. The molds used by Talmage and Wesley rarely suit the new age—but their gospel of the unbounding love of God is ever the same.

We have undoubtedly heard some description such as the following:

In the midst of a great storm (the details of which are elaborated upon at length), a little boy becomes terrified and, climbing out of his berth, makes his way perilously to the pilothouse where the captain is at the wheel. The brawny man takes one hand from the wheel and places a strong arm about the frightened child. As the ship lurches in the howling wind and mighty waves, the captain says, "Son, go back to your cabin and go to sleep. Father will guide the ship safely through the storm." Calmed and reassured, the child goes back to his bed and to sleep. When morning breaks, the child awakes to find the ship gently swaying on a calm sea, and through the porthole he looks upon the quiet sea and a bright blue sky above. His father has brought the ship safely through the troubled night.

This type of illustration is long out of date, especially among younger people—if it did not always carry too heavy a load of doubt as to its authenticity.

It has been suggested that we search the world for our symbols and examples, ancient as well as modern. And that is still pertinent advice; but let those we use be fresh, vigorous, clear, unhampered by the staleness of familiarity.

Use No Counterfeits

Persons attended church in days gone by in no small part because the minister was the one person in the community who was well informed. He had information in various fields and upon subjects of the day about which they knew nothing except as they learned at church. But how many people attend your church because you are the best informed person in the community, or because you are the only source of contemporary knowledge to which they may turn? The probability is that some person in the congregation knows at least as much, if not more, about each of the items upon which you speak, as you do. This is a day of specialization and some technician or student will be on hand to check on your authority. And many of the persons of humble origin or occupation may through reading or travel be completely familiar with sights and sounds and far-away places.

A plumber in a little Kentucky town had traveled with his wife around the world. In the same community an engineer was a master of bird life in the South; a teacher in the high school was unusually well versed in the lore of Lincoln, and had a garden with over one hundred varieties of iris; a lawyer had followed his Browning hobby until he probably knew what Browning meant in some instances better than the poet himself; and every high school student had more information about the earth, the heavens, and the nations than philosophers, kings, and wise men of old. In a little Southeast Missouri town a Methodist congregation of 240 members contains forty-two persons who have attended or graduated from college.

Whenever a preacher speaks before such a congregation as is gathered in any city or hamlet or even in the country-side, he has a critical audience. His speech will of necessity be "yea, yea" or "nay, nay," and whatsoever is more than this will be heard with reservations. More fundamental to the minister than that the congregation may detect him should be his unfailing purpose to have his sermon in every part, illustrations and all else, true to fact. We wish to become "all things to all men," but this does not include the fault of exaggeration.

A true minister will spare himself no effort to ascertain the facts. The following is an oft-quoted story.

"We sing sometimes that hymn of Matheson's, 'O Love that wilt not let me go.' But it is worth-while to remember how Matheson came to write those beautiful lines. Nay, we need to know how he came to the experience out of which he could write them. He had loved a woman as only a fine-grained man can ever love. But when blindness came upon him the woman gave him up. Her renouncement broke his heart, but it drove him to the heart of One who *would not let him go*. And so he sang of what he had found: 'O Love that wilt not let me go.' " [16]

It is easy to ascertain the facts in this case, which are that this story is false.[17] Matheson became blind at the age of fifteen and wrote the hymn at the age of forty. He tells in his own words how it was written—in a far more deeply spiritual experience than the sentimental story quoted above. A preacher must be exceedingly careful to ascertain the truth, the whole truth, and not leave a question about his integrity.

Since no preacher is omniscient, even the youngest of us, at his best he is apt to err. It would increase the appreciation of his future messages if he would acknowledge any error.

The preacher does not always realize how critical are some of the members of his congregation, or how some little question about an incidental illustration may ruin the entire sermon for some person.

One Sunday night I told a story which I had heard several years before from my parents who had gone into the Yukon Territory of Northwestern Canada in the gold rush of 1898. I do not now remember what it illustrated, but here is the story: "The Yukon River at that time was the only way into the Klondike and the travelers had to go down it by boat. Their boat had been handmade at the headwaters and was large enough to carry a year's provisions for the two of them. At one place in the journey the river, as wide as the Ohio below Louisville, narrowed into a gorge known as Miles Canyon, where the waters were compressed between high stone walls into a torrent not over 150 feet across. The water rushing through this narrow gorge was several feet higher in the center than at the sides. Those in the boats had to row faster than the current to keep from being dashed to pieces against the rock walls."

A half dozen young married couples had the habit of sitting together on Sunday nights and afterwards going to someone's home for refreshments (which I suppose they needed) and where they sat about and talked. The day after this illustration was used I met one of the young men down town. He said, "Say, preacher, we talked about your sermon last night and agreed that that was a tall story you told about that great river narrowing down into such a little gorge. You couldn't get that much water through such a small canyon."

I was chagrined and told him it had been several years since I had heard it and that it was possible the dimensions had been unintentionally exaggerated, but I would look it up to be sure. Several months previously the *National Geographic Magazine* had contained a story about two men who had recently followed the old Yukon trail. I located the magazine, which previously I had gone through hurriedly, and sure enough, there was the story and the picture of Miles Canyon, exactly as I had described it.

That made a considerable impression on me—not that I had been accurate in this instance and had the vain privilege of saying to my friend, "I told you so," but that I must endeavor to be as nearly correct as possible in every detail in every illustration of the future. And further, that I should give the care to finding the facts before, rather than after, the sermon. "Be as imaginative as possible, but discerning and truthful withal." [18]

Siamese Twins

Occasionally in nature there is a phenomenon, rare but of unusual interest, where twins are born, not separate and distinct in body but joined together physically. They must accompany each other throughout life, and yet each seems to be a distinct personality, intellectually competent, with differing thoughts and often differing desires. While they are physically a unit they are two personalities.

There is a phenomenon of sermonic illustration, not so rare as in nature, but equally interesting and valuable, where a single illustration contains two personalities. It may fit perfectly at the point at issue and yet be as well a reinforcement to some other equally important phase of the Christian gospel.

Scriptural illustrations, besides carrying the point for which they are selected, will increase the hearer's knowledge and appreciation of the Bible. Instances from the lives and events of the mission fields not only may indicate types of character and attitudes toward life, but also provide a background of missionary philosophy. Out of this there will come later prayers, attitudes of brotherly good will overcoming racial and social barriers, and probably contributions to the missionary enterprises. It is not the frontal attack so much as the flank movement which is successful in preaching. This is particularly true in helping one's people to meet the economic, social, international, and temperance problems. A sermon on intemperance is not nearly so valuable as illustrations of the effects of both temperance and intemperance, used with more or less frequency, in sermons which seem to be dealing with entirely different matters.

A preacher might be speaking on the conservation of those abilities, talents, and material resources which are God-given. In the sermon he could use the following from Victor Berger, former member of Congress from Wisconsin.

"The World War, all told, cost—apart from 30,000,000 lives—$400,000,000,000 in property. With that money we could have built a $2,500 house, furnished it with $1,000 worth of furniture, placed it on five acres of land worth $100 an acre, and given this home to each and every family in the United States, Canada, Australia, England, Wales, Ireland, Scotland, France, Belgium, Germany, and Russia. We could have given to each city of 20,000 inhabitants and over, in each country named, a $5,000,000 library, a $5,000,000 hospital, and a $10,000,000 university. Out of what was left over we could have set aside a sum at five per cent interest that would provide a $1,000 yearly salary for an army of 125,000 teachers and a like salary for another army of 125,-000 nurses." [19]

In using this statement he would indict the waste of God-given resources in no uncertain terms and also would give a far greater indictment of war. That illustration alone might convert some person to opposition to war, and would certainly plant a seed of distrust in everyone's mind about an institution which would so totally destroy valuable God-given possessions.

A surprising justification for the above paragraphs, which were written several weeks ago, came this morning. I just received a long-distance telephone call from a layman in a church where I had used the above quotation in the way indicated above. In the phone call he said, "You preached in our church a couple of months ago giving a statement of the terrific cost of the World War. I told my daughter about it. She has just written me from college saying she is to give a talk on the futility of war and wants the facts you quoted if you still have them." I have no way of knowing if my principal point in the sermon was remembered by this layman, but it is evident that its twin, the futility of war, made its impression.

When a preacher has to choose between two illustrations which he may use with equal effectiveness in a particular sermon, he will gain by selecting that one which will give the largest possible application to the entire Christian message, the one which carries double personality.

Unselfish Pictures

Unselfishness is a Christian virtue and it may well be a cardinal one for an illustration. Illuminative material is not in the sermon for its own glory. It is not to attract attention to itself, although it may be most attractive; it is not there for its brilliance, although it may be bright; it is not used to startle, although it may be starkly real; but it is there to help people to see the TRUTH.

Windows are not put into houses for their own sake, but to give light. Illustrations are not in sermons because they have particular beauty and attractiveness, but to illuminate the principles of our teaching. There are occasionally windows in houses which are evidently placed there to call attention to themselves and, occasionally, there are illustrations in some sermons which seem to indicate the same selfishness.

Whenever a man says to a woman, "What a lovely hat you are wearing," it is no complement to the woman and she had better get another hat. But when she has bought a new hat or outfit and he exclaims, "How lovely you look," the hat and clothes are a success.

One critical question a preacher may rightly ask of every aid to his preaching, "Are you here for your own glory or do you lend winsomeness and beauty and vitality to my message?" If the former, it has no place in his sermon; if the latter, then it is an ally of God and the preacher's collaborator.

It has been said that if one is impatient to use a new illustration for the sake of its beauty, its novelty, or its cleverness, he had better "salt it down in the notebook till it is entirely apt." [20]

REPETITION!

The danger of repetition of thought is not serious. The people easily forget your line of reasoning. Ah! but repetition of your stories is fatal! They are so easily remembered. As a boy attending church (and I am thankful that my parents, lay people, always took me), how tired I would get when the preacher again came to one of his favorite stories, which by now I could tell as well as he, except for the enlargement his imagination sometimes gave.

A young preacher in Kentucky has a file in which he carefully indexes all his illustrative material. He prepares his sermons with the file immediately in front of him, and when he desires an illustration, he searches until the proper one is found, and then drags it out, puts it into his sermon—no matter how often it has been used before. "If it fits, it fits," he says, "and that is all there is to it." That is all, except that to his preaching it is as a fatal disease, and to the congregation increasingly painful.

How a man is to keep from repeating is no easy matter to settle. He must remember what he has used, or he must take from his file or mark out of his notebook that which has been told once. He must—or else invite ruin.

A layman was asked by the presiding elder about the advisability of a certain pastor's return for the coming year. The layman replied: "Our pastor is all right, and I believe he should return, although he could study more. But I certainly wish he would stop telling so often that story about the little black mule."

If you have any doubt as to how easily illustrations are remembered in contrast to abstract thought, if you have courage and are able to stand disappointment, ask some member of your congregation what you preached about Sunday before last. Then ask him if he remembers any illustrations. In all likelihood he will remember the incidents you used (if they were used), and can reconstruct your argument around those illustrations.

If you do not want to go through that probably painful process, turn to the preaching of Jesus. Try to recall immediately four *abstract* statements Jesus made about God's relation to man. At last, after some thought, you have them. Now try to recall four stories or pictures Jesus used concerning God's relation to man—and see the symbols and stories crowd for place: Shepherd, the Prodigal's Father, the Judge, the woman seeking a coin, bread and not a stone, the Great Physician, the Cross.

However you keep from it, never repeat an illustration.

BE A PLAGIARIST

There is much discussion as to the right of a minister to use material which has come from sources other than his own brain and personal experience. A sermon which had its origin entirely in the author would be—a blank; or so nearly so that few would recognize the difference.

Contrast the sermon without illustrations, or the one with only those of personal experience, with one which comes out of the entire Christian experience of the ages, "encompassed with so great a cloud of witnesses," and you have inane boredom as against eagle-winged animation.

"Be a plagiarist" is excellent advice to any preacher when it comes to illustrations. Get whatever you can and all you can, wherever you can—nature, books, the congregation, the Bible, everywhere. Whenever it is necessary to give a reference, do so. But it is not always necessary.

A young minister was the platform speaker at a young people's summer assembly. He had brilliant illustrations and numerous quotations. At the conclusion of one of his addresses a young person remarked, "His messages are helpful, but I get so distracted by his mention of Dr. So-and-So, Professor Whatnot, and the eminent writer Whosit."

In contrast recently a prominent minister in a sermon told a story without any reference as to where it came from. I knew where he got it, as I had read it before. As he was preaching, the congregation knew it was not his personal experience. He made no attempt to leave that impression; he knew and everyone else knew that he was not trying to pass it off as something original. But I was glad that at that important moment in the message he did not force in the annotations of where, when, and under what circumstances that illustration had come to him. Any reference at that moment would have weakened his sermon.

The preacher is delivering a sermon and not writing a book or article with appended footnotes. And even in the bookmaker's art, footnotes are often added in the end of the book where those desiring may find them. They do not clutter the reading matter where one wants to follow more closely the argument.

Illustrations are common property and it is seldom necessary or advisable to give the source.

There are a few ministers who themselves are poets. They should indicate that the quoted verse is not their own. But for the vast majority of us we need not tell, unless we want to use the name of the author for the strength it will add, that the poem about to be used came from some renowned or well-known muse. The congregation will be well aware that is was not original.

And yet in so far as you can, acknowledge your sources. "If you borrow deliberately, admit it deliberately." [21]

There is a grace in introducing the sources or the persons quoted. Dr. Frederick Fisher does it with consummate skill as in the following: "Our greatest poet of modern science, Alfred Noyes . . ." "Chinese Gordon, that marvelous old military leader in China and Egypt, . . ." "Bliss Carman, who lives under the elms of Cambridge in Harvard's easy environment . . ." "Jerome K. Jerome, in his *Passing of the Third Floor Back* (a book that might properly be regarded as a modern Gospel), gives a picture of Christ . . ." "I close with glorious Robert Browning . . ." Dr. Fisher intrigues you to want to know those whom he knows. With his short descriptive phrase, he opens a window into the soul of some person. "Walter Rauschenbusch, founder of modern Christian sociology, who in many ways was its deepest scholar and its finest personal exponent, whose social soul was so highly sensitized that when the war came he died of a broken heart, who could not endure the violent break-up of the social order, having given his intellectual and spiritual soul so deeply to that cause, Walter Rauschenbusch said, in a beautiful little poem, 'The Gate to God':

> 'In the castle of my soul
> Is a little postern gate,
> Whereat, when I enter,
> I am in the presence of God
> In a moment, in the turning of a thought,
> I am where God is.
> This is a fact.' " [22]

195

Stories and incidents may be told without any acknowledgment, except that events which did not happen to the speaker must never be indicated as personal experiences. Illustrations may be freely used without stating sources. But thoughts, ideas, descriptions, particularly if over a line or two, if incorporated in a sermon, must never, in all fairness, be pawned off as one's own. While illustrations may become common property, ideas are not.

Dr. Lynn Harold Hough has this paragraph in the early part of a sermon on "Finding Our Way in the Twentieth Century": "It is not strange that a world containing the phenomena to which we referred should become a world of vast disillusionment at last. And at this point the witness is clear. Progress has gone forward. Our emancipations have not set us free. 'We have substituted trivial illusions for magnificent faiths,' says Walter Lippmann. Paul Valery from his intellectual throne admits that the Western mind is characterized by contradictory ideas and incompatible desires. 'Ours is a lost cause,' declares Joseph Wood Krutch in words of mordant honesty. And Mrs. Virginia Wolff sees a typical artist doing meticulously careful work in almost utter darkness." [23] This of course is not the conclusion of his sermon, which does end: "So the threads of the keenest thought, scientific and philosophic, and of that thought which makes its way through all the manifold expressions in literary form of the human spirit, comes together at last. And so the signs of the times point to personality free and responsible as the only certainty in this baffling world. And when critical faith takes the leap of venturing to believe in God . . ." In the quotations of ideas here made, the authors are clearly indicated.

Any quotation of thought or argument, if taken directly from another, even though it has been run through the mill of one's own mind, for all honesty's sake, must be acknowledged.

The late Dr. S. Parkes Cadman gives good advice: "Do not vex yourself about originality, for Emerson laid that specter when he said that all literature since Plato was a quotation. You cannot turn to an essay of the Sage of Concord without finding numerous citations from the best works. His frequency and suitability in appropriating the words of earlier writers provoked the comment of Oliver Wendell Holmes, that Emerson's quotations were like the miraculous draught of fishes." [24]

Abbe Bautain states the case pertinently: "The fund to be amassed by those who intend to speak in public is a treasury of ideas, thoughts, and principles of knowledge, strongly conceived, firmly linked together, carefully thought out, in such a way that, throughout all this diversity of study, the mind, so far as may be, shall admit nothing save what it thoroughly comprehends, or at least has made its own to a certain extent by meditation." [25]

The advice we would give is to be a plagiarist—an honest one. Lay tribute to the whole world, acknowledge what you must in good conscience and for the greatest effectiveness of your sermons.

VIII

COMPOSING THE ILLUSTRATION

MUCH of the effectiveness of an illustration is produced by the composition—often as much as by the incident itself. An example dawdled over, poorly formed in thought, slovenly expressed in wording, or vagrant in conclusion will be ruinous, whatever be its other merits.

Considerable attention must be given in the study to the literary style and arrangement of the dress in which the instance is to be clothed. No one can approach the stories of Jesus without marveling at their beauty, effectiveness of style, and masterful pithiness. While we do not know the thought processes which the Master had, we may well be assured from the resultant art that he made his mind walk the straight and narrow path out of which alone could come such perfect illuminations of the faith. We would profit by regulating our life in the hours of study so that the same results might be approached in our own preaching. It is an experiment worth while in itself to examine the sermons of the great preachers in this one regard—namely, the arrangement and formation of the illustration itself.

COMPOSING THE ILLUSTRATION

Introducing the Illustration

We are not considering here the instance which opens a sermon, but the ways in which the illustration may be most effectively and without jar brought into its proper place in the discourse.

It is usually best to have little or no preface at all. If it can be done without a break in thought, it is wise to begin at once with the example. The introduction of author, title, and chapter usually has a deadening effect, and, because of such, many an otherwise good illustration is brought forth stillborn.

It is usually best to slip in the case in point as informally as possible.

The following examples are given to indicate that there may be a great variety in the opening wording of the illustration:

"There is a most revealing story of a president of a large American University and one of his professors. . . ." [1] "There is a fascinating story. . . ." [2] "Let us begin with a rare old tradition. . . ." [3] "But perhaps we moderns, with our wireless and our radio, have an even more striking illustration of such spiritual understanding. . . ." [4] "Here is a roadside experience taken from the paper which gives vividness to what I mean. . . ." [5] "Perhaps you will get this distinction best by a single illustration adapted from one Hutchinson uses in *The Uncertain Trumpet*. My adaptation is as follows. . . ." [6] "There was once a thrill of strange excitement in Auburn prison. . . ." [7] "Francis Thompson's con-

fession is a poetic description of the inescapable Christ. . . ." [8]
"Let me impress my message with a familiar story. . . ." [9]

A minister might well practice in his study a variety of ways in which he could introduce the same incident, finally choosing the one which most nearly adapted itself to the sermon in hand, and the one which had been most rarely used by himself in the past.

"STYLE IS THE DRESS OF THOUGHTS"

Something has already been said about the style of illustrations, the value of stating the case so that it will be most attractive. Perhaps too much can be said about it, but it is certain that too much attention cannot be given by the preacher to choice of expression.

Simplicity of style, with wording striking and impressionistic, is to be coveted. It requires movement, vitality, aliveness, but unity withal; variety for the individual parts but unity for the whole composition. Mrs. F. A. Clifford, founder of the St. Louis Storytellers' League, impresses upon her pupils, many of whom are most excellent and delightful storytellers, that the highest art in relating stories is simplicity, both of matter and of presentation. The preacher will find valuable help in studying the impressionistic school of painting. Words, like preachers, may be lazily employed, and the man who would preach should see to it that words work diligently and effectively for him.

When a minister finds a written illustration which he would use in his sermon, he is faced with the question, "How shall I use it, verbatim or in different form?" And the answer depends entirely upon the use to which he is to put it. Sometimes an example is so concisely and interestingly written that it could not be improved upon. In which case he will want to use it as he finds it.

Often, however, the illustration may be reworked so as to fit more indigenously and smoothly into the sermon. It might be better introduced, or irrelevant parts omitted, or the climax readjusted. A man has a perfect liberty to rework an illustration to suit his need in so far as he does not distort or prejudice the facts.

Again there are times when only the basic facts are given and the preacher is justified in imaginatively filling in the spaces. Every preacher has done this with some passage of Scripture such as the story of the lost sheep. The use to which he puts an illustration and the result he will expect from it will determine whether he will tell it as found or in better form. His right to change the fashion is solely his own so long as he does not twist or falsify the original and basic circumstances. The congregation must always be aware that their preacher is sincere, particularly in the veracity of his illustrations. To quote or not to quote verbatim is a question each minister must answer in each individual case for himself.

THE FORM

The form in which the illustration appears is exceedingly important and often is as valuable to the hearer's interest as the example itself. The influence of the sermon may be largely increased by the use of varied and different forms for the illuminative material. The same instance may be dressed in any one of a number of varying styles.

NARRATION

The simplest form is the narrative in which a succession of events occurs, sometimes covering several years, as the life unfolds itself. It may be a brief narrative of a day or a week in a person's experience. The secret is that the story shows movement and reality and comes to a definite conclusion. It dare not trail off into the trivial or unimportant. It must come to grips with life.

The following narrative incident is well told for sermonic purposes:

"On the Labrador coast one day Dr. Grenfell was called to see a dying girl who had been cooking and mending for the men in one of the small fishing huts. He found her in a rude bunk, dying with typhoid fever, her only nurse an old sea captain. The old man held the lamp while the doctor did all he could to give the girl ease, but the captain was very downhearted and slipped out every now and again into the dark as though watching for something. That night the girl died, and after the burial the doctor helped the captain to carry her bunk and belongings, and on to the edge of the cliff a bonfire was made to prevent the carrying of infection. As the flames leaped up the doctor learned the cause of the captain's anxiety—a big boat, with his sons on board, had been missing since the morning in the fog. Before he left next day, the doctor had the joy of seeing the missing boat return with the captain's sons safe and sound. He found then that the girl's death had been the means of saving the lives of the boat's crew, for that bonfire on the cliff had been a beacon shining through the darkness and fog, giving the lost boat the one signal they needed to work their way back to their island home." [10]

DESCRIPTION

Similar to the narrative is description of scene, character, or mental state. There is a grave danger that the description may take up too large a part of the sermon. Settings of Bible scenes cannot be as long and detailed for the modern movie-minded as for a bygone patient generation. Such descriptions must be given in bold strokes which kindle the imagination of the hearer to fill in for himself the body of that setting. The description of mental states from a modern psychological point of view is often a necessity, that the people may know whereof they are made and the forces against which they fight with the resources of mind and spirit which religion brings to their command. Much valuable assistance can be given to troubled souls by analyzing difficulties and conflicts. And yet such descriptions need to be given, not in the words of psychologist and psychiatrist, but in popular, understandable terms. Such an analysis as the following is not only accurate but has curative and healing powers:

"Here is a boy born a cripple or crippled in early infancy; he has grown up through his first years with no idea of what has happened to him, but sometime in childhood it will dawn on him that he is not like other children, that he has a handicap. His spiritual problem will center in the way he deals with that. Or here is a man whose parents did not understand the critical importance of the emotional experiences of childhood, who now wakes up to discover that something is wrong inside, that all his basic, habitual emotional reactions flow in channels of suspicion, distrust, fear, anxiety, and vindictiveness, so that like a stream in endless agitation he looks in envy at smoothly-flowing personalities that can maintain a tranquil, deep, even course. That man's spiritual problem will center in the vicinity of his handicap.

"Or here is a man who in youth had all the natural ambitions of young manhood for success but who now recognizes that he never will arrive at his desired goal. He will never write the poetry or compose the music or preach the sermons or hold the business positions that he dreamed. Again and again he has stepped on the gas, but the speed is not in him. Nature did not equip him with eight cylinders or with six— only four, and those none too good. It is a crucial hour in that man's life when he stands open-eyed before his handicap. . . .

"Moreover, there are some whose limitations lie in personal relationships—a life that wanted love and missed it, a home where marriage might have been a thing of beauty but was a tragedy, a family where a child was greeted as a blessing but became an inward agony, a household where death has severed a tie that was the support and glory of the home. Among the few things that are true of all of us is the fact that each one has a handicap." [11]

DIALOGUE

Again it is possible to arrange the incident in the form of a dialogue. This is a most interesting and appealing method of preaching. Like the drama it must be lifelike and dramatic. The type of conversation found in Job is probably too involved for our day, but pithy conversation is powerful and effective.

The old elocution has long since passed out of the picture, and yet there is a place for sane depiction of character. Each minister must decide for himself the extent to which he, with his own talents and abilities, can represent various other persons in conversation. Dialogue can often be represented realistically with simply the turn of the head, the inflection of the voice, or a plain statement as to who is speaking.

The use of dialect, brogue, or speech peculiar to any class or race, trade, or profession, will depend both upon the ability of the speaker to use it naturally and also upon the point of the sermon where it is brought in.

Marc Connelly epitomizes the gospel in the closing scene of the play, "The Green Pastures," which made such a profound religious impression upon the nation. This scene is a powerful representation for a sermon if the preacher can use it naturally and sincerely.

God is seated in an armchair surrounded by angels. The following conversation takes place between God and Gabriel:

Gabriel. "You look pensive, Lawd. You been sittin' yere lookin' dis way an awful long time. Is it somethin' serious, Lawd?"

"Very serious, Gabriel."

"Lawd, is de time come for me to blow?"

"Not yet, Gabriel. I'm just thinkin'."

"What about, Lawd?"

"'Bout somethin' that boy tole me. Somethin' bout Hosea and himself. How dey foun' somethin'."

"What, Lawd?"

"*Mercy . . through sufferin'*, he said."

"Yes, Lawd."

"I'm tryin' to find it too. It's awful impo'tant. It's awful impo'tant to all de people on my earth. Did dat mean that even God must suffer?"

In the distance a voice cries—"Oh, look at him! Oh, look, dey goin' to make him carry it up dat high hill! Dey goin' to nail him to it! Oh, dat's a terrible burden for one man to carry."

God rises and murmurs, "Yes," as if in recognition.[12]

The attempt to use this dialogue should be made only after a minister is certain he could do it naturally and sincerely There are many white ministers who can use negro dialect with naturalness and force, but on the other hand there are many others who should never attempt it. Recently I heard a man in the pulpit try to imitate a conversation between negroes. It was quite evident that neither by association with people of the negro race nor by any natural or cultivated talent of his own could he in the least represent their mode of speech. What he did was to make an unintentional farce of what should have been a deeply spiritual experience. It would have been much better if he had told the experience of these two colored people in his own manner without any attempt to imitate their style.

Again there are situations so serious in the sermon that dialogue, other than the manner of the speaker, is entirely out of place. There are occasions when its use calls attention to itself rather than to the matter being considered. At any point it must be given simply, with unaffected sincerity. Real care should be exercised that the preacher who impersonates any other person does so with understanding, love, and fidelity. Dialogue can be used with variety, is refreshing to the congregation, and has immense practical value.

BIOGRAPHY

Biography or autobiography is another form the illustration may take. Since preaching is "truth through personality," it is probably the experiences which come through the fire of one's own ministry which are the most valid to the sermon. We are all as listeners far more interested in the description of an eyewitness than in echoed reports. The actual experience in which a minister met someone in difficulty is far more helpful and satisfying to a person in trouble than secondhand advice. Of course the danger is that the sermon may tend to become a big "I," in which case the congregation soon feel that religion has narrowed to the smallest word in the English language. At times illustrations can be autobiographical, and also real and experimentally religious. A minister who can use the happenings from his own life without the congregation thinking that he is giving merely a running commentary on a not-too-interesting life has the advantage of focalizing his message into near-to-home experiences.

Or he may use the biographical method to present the views, reports, adventures, and fortunes of others than himself. It is possible to take a character from Scripture, from history, or a living person, and present the situation or mental state as that one sees it.

Dr. Clovis Chappell takes a text from Scripture and delineates it in personal terms of the author. The text is "Come and hear, all ye that fear God, and I will declare what he hath done for my soul." He begins, "Here is a man who is determined to get a hearing. He has a story to tell that simply will not keep. He must share it with others. He has an eye more compelling than that of the Ancient Mariner. Not only so, but he seems to throw all timidity to the winds as he hurries to lay eager hands on any chance passer-by that he may constrain him to hear his story. He even reaches those eager hands far across the centuries and puts them upon our listless and preoccupied souls and undertakes to shape us into wakefulness and expectancy . . ." [13]

BALANCED THOUGHT

Then there is the balanced illustration. It contrasts between two opposing conditions of life: the evil and the good; right and wrong; the eternal tension of soul with matter; and the possible solution through spiritual power. The following is an excellent example of such a balanced picturization:

"Some, however, go to pieces. Here is one man who becomes cynical. He curses life, calls it an aimless, footless misadventure into which it is a disaster ever to have been born. As we hear him talking so, we say to ourselves, He is going to pieces. It may be, however, that later we hear him speak again: I made up my mind that cynicism was not getting me anywhere; that, after all, there are some things in human life to believe in; I have gotten a new grip on faith and it is faith in something that makes life worth living. And we say, He has found something that is pulling him together again.

"Or here is a man who becomes hopeless and thinks he is done for, saying, as one person in the twenties said to me only this last week, 'I am finished—nothing ahead.' Noting such hopelessness, one says, He is going to pieces. But later, it may be, we meet that man again and he says: 'After all, no man is finally defeated until he thinks he is; it is hope which essentially makes a personality with power to throw an aim ahead and then hurl himself after it; I made up my mind that I would not quit being a person; I actually have recovered hope.' And we say, He has found something that is pulling him together again." [14]

These illustrations tell of men who have lost all hope but who now have caught hold of the eternal which brings life back. How often this type of example is used by preachers because it is of the essence of the Christian religion! That which was lost is saved, whether it be an individual or a nation. In a world order such as the present where we see on every hand nations, cultures, economic orders, and religious faiths collapsing, there is yet the regenerative power of Christ which alone can renew and implement for a new day. Such illustrations of conversion from the old to the new will always be of inestimable value to the preacher.

THE DRAMATIC

Practically every illustration should be as technically perfect in form as a short story. Material normally uninteresting may be worked into the dramatic without losing any value as truth or without distorting the facts. Whatever its form otherwise, as narrative, conversation, biography, it should be shaped to follow this sequence: build up the interest, reach a climax, and clinch the point in the closing moments. This is essential if the illustration is to have pertinence and permanence.

Watch this concluding illustration of a sermon by Dr. Merton S. Rice as it builds up from merely a curiosity attached to a name, through interest that quickly intensifies, and then comes to a dramatic and satisfying climax:

"How eagerly we should lift our imperfect lives to the great fulfillment of God's ultimate purpose," is the final statement immediately reinforced with this illustration: "The story of Fritz Kreisler and his insistent pursuit of the great violin which had become the mute possession of a great collector of violins, is known everywhere. The artist could not rest while that wonderful instrument was a mere curio. One day, after repeated requests, the owner in a fit of desperation granted the violinist the opportunity to play upon it. He played as he had never played before. He said he played as though to ransom a slave. When at last in trembling loveliness the tones died away the owner said, in great emotion, 'It belongs to you, sir. I have no right to keep it here. Take it. Play on it. Go to the world with it and let it be heard.'" [15]

The Application

There is considerable argument on both sides as to whether an application should be made at the conclusion of an apt illustration. It is usually best to make the application first and follow it with the illumination. Each instance must meet this test of itself in the preacher's mind: Does this example carry its own tidings or must I add a statement or so to enforce it?

In a discourse to persuade, which preaching is, the minister does well to energetically apply to the fullest degree. I have on occasion come away from some message by an eminent preacher with the realization that he had pressed out of his illustrations the fullest measure of juice—and with what variety and skill.

Following the illustration just quoted above about Kreisler

and the violin, Dr. Rice goes on to gain the value of his argument and the incident with this appeal: "O thou unstrung soul! You may be now shut away from your best by so much in life that has muted you to all your powers! God is thine only perfection: 'I shall be satisfied, when I awake, with thy likeness.' Know thy destiny. 'When that which is perfect is come.' Look ahead of thee there. It is coming!" [16]

As with children, it is usually and in most instances best to leave the illustration while it still suggests something more than what has actually been expressed. The imagination of the hearer is a powerful ally of the preacher, and he can well expect its assistance in making the application without added words on his part. The prosaic words of the preacher might be stifling, while it is possible that the hearer will take the suggestion of the story and suit it to himself imaginatively and in more realistic fashion. The acceptable rule to follow, as with Jesus, is—let the illustration carry its own truth.

The danger, however, is that many people are so prosaically minded that they will not see the point. But there are occasions when we must paint the picture and then let those who have eyes see and ears hear, knowing full well that there are others present "who, having ears, hear not, and having eyes, see not."

The primary value of letting the example carry its own word is that it is capable of varied and continuous application.

How well I remember the first time in my ministry when I found that one of my congregation had been creatively caught hold of by an illustration. In attempting to gain a larger liberality toward the enterprises of the Kingdom, I had presented an illustration intended to make real the question of Malachi, "Will a man rob God?" The following morning I met a member of my flock, a merchant, who said, "That story you told yesterday surely hit me. Last week I sold a man a floor lamp for his wife, representing to him that it was first-class workmanship at a most reasonable price. It really was a cheap price, but it was also a cheap article. That story you told made me feel that I had done wrong."

My first impression was that the sermon of that morning had not produced the expected results. I had failed to make my point clear: that a man should not rob God. But on second thought I realized that the illustration had succeeded far better than I had planned. It had a wider and more personal application than any mere abstract statement. Had not that merchant in reality learned something inestimable about devotion to God?

The widening application of some example is apparent when we think of the parables of the Master which yield with every generation and each succeeding age an ever-increasing return. As illustrations stir the imagination of the hearers, they create individual and personal meaning not contained in the original thoughts of the speaker. Each instance should be weighed to determine if application should be made or if it should carry its own message.

We have gathered our illustrative materials, preserved them until the time of need, and in that necessity built them into the sermon; now let us consider methods of presentation.

THE STORY METHOD OF PREACHING

A LAYMAN was speaking with his pastor concerning the minister of a neighboring church and giving his reason for the large congregations attending there. Said he: "He is a good storyteller; and, frankly, I think you tell too few."

This statement was intended as a compliment to the effectiveness of the other preacher and as a constructive criticism of his own minister, whom he admired greatly. In reality, however, it might have been proscribing judgment upon the real failure of the other preacher. For it all depends upon what the stories are, how they are used and their spiritual effect upon the lives of the people. The fact that people listen or hear with pleasure or even attend in large numbers is no guarantee of good consequences. Children and grown-up children love stories—with or without point. How hard it is for the gifted illustrator to enter that kingdom of spiritual influence where people follow his guidance in living, daily conduct! Yet this is the final test.

The preacher was more severe in his self-criticism when, acknowledging his layman's correct analysis, he said, "He

does illustrate his sermons well, but I find that it takes hard work." An honest reply, but is that an excuse?

We may not disparage the storyteller with the diatribe that he replaces reason by imagination if we respect Jesus. For no preacher ever invented or used more powerful verbal pictures than He. And yet with what reason! Never an irrelevant phrase, much less an immaterial or ill-spent story; never an illustration for its own sake or even to create interest. Always he used them with one purpose, spiritual revelation.

What we need in our pulpits is more and better "storytellers," those who reveal the realities of the Kingdom with creative imagination. In sermons the story feature can well be employed with greater frequency. It lends variety, carries the audience with it, stimulates their thinking, is less likely to be abstract in form, is usually of a lifelike situation, and indirectly leads to concrete action. These advantages, of course, come only when the story is rightly used.

A Means of Changing Conduct

The primary purpose of preaching is changed living. There is no other method which can so effectively redeem conduct as that of the story.

A nationally known coach stated recently that when a football team recognizes its own ability and feels itself confident of winning the next game with an inferior foe, there is no amount of advice the coach can give to counteract the overconfidence. The players cannot be convinced that the

opposing team is keyed-up for that game and is likely to give such stiff competition that it may possibly win. They *know* better. Advice is not enough. It seems the only way for them to find out, said he, is to be defeated by their own over-confidence.

Advice is not enough in the pulpit. There must be conviction. Some few will take advice, but the majority, the vast majority, must have their desires and purposes stirred and their emotional set changed. In spite of the fact that people have the information concerning the overpowering strength of evil, they know better—until in the contest they are defeated. The story is particularly effective and probably the only method of attaining this realization. It becomes a project, entered into emotionally by the hearer, until he associates himself creatively in the action of the participants. In the crisis which a person faces, the story enables him to analyze his situation, to feel that he is not alone in it, to find a workable solution, which, if previously proven reasonable, now has emotional content and impelling force.

There is real justification for the use of stories in sermons. Stories develop Christlike attitudes, form purposes that will lead to higher ideals, challenge hearers to build new habits that will enrich life, lead to better personal living and a finer existence for the world.

Every one of us knows from his own experience that when a story is being told he enters imaginatively into the characters. He feels as though he were acting as the hero; he despises the wrongdoer, and desires the undoing of the

216

wrong; he rejoices at triumph of good and sorrows when evil befalls; he *feels* his own ideals lifted when he hears of someone who has proved faithful and courageous. Every one of us at some time has become a better man or woman because he has entered imaginatively and creatively into the lifting power of some story.

Margaret Eggleston, who has had results of inestimable value in telling stories to girls, makes this observation: "The teen-age girl is a great problem and at the same time a great opportunity. Her ideals seem low, yet there is no time in her life when she will more gladly follow a great ideal. . . . Her problems are many, and most of them she must solve alone. If she follows the crowd and goes in the way of least resistance, there is a big chance that she will fall by the way. If she does not follow the crowd, it is because somewhere, sometime, she has found a compelling ideal and is following it. . . . Often and often it comes to her through a little story that lives with her, and works for her, and helps her to hold to her best, in spite of the manifold temptations to do otherwise." She illustrates the statement with the following: "Recently I met a young woman whom I had seen only once and that was twelve years ago. She came to me after a service and said, 'Will you tell Van Dyke's "Lump of Clay" tonight? Twelve years ago I heard you tell it. I was so discouraged at the time, for everything seemed going wrong and life seemed so useless. But I dropped into a church and heard you tell the story. You have no idea what it has done for me. I am teaching in the college near by and I

should like to have my girls hear the story. Perhaps they need it as I did.' " [1]

If a preacher can tell a story which can so affect the life of a young woman or young man in his congregation, his sermon has found its mark. And how Christlike has become his ministry! If he feels no compulsion to minister through life-giving stories in his regular preaching, where is the compassion which Jesus showed to all the multitudes, youth as well as age?

THE FOCAL POINT

A preacher may discuss theoretically the reality of first-hand knowledge concerning God. He may expound the doctrine to the full, which is to be encouraged rather than discounted, yet the final and focal point of what that means can be made truly real by the citation of some individual person to whom it has become authentic.

The following would certainly bring into apprehension the experimental content of knowing God: "It is said that one day in London an atheist sought to make sport of an unlettered man who had been converted only a short time before. 'Do you know anything about Jesus Christ?' he asked. 'Yes, by the grace of God, I do,' was the answer. 'When was he born?' was the next question. The ignorant saint gave an incorrect answer. 'How old was he when he died?' Again the answer was incorrect. Other questions were asked with the same result until the atheist said with a sneer, 'See, you do not know so much about Jesus as you thought, do you?' 'I know all too little,' was the modest reply, 'but I know this:

I was one of the worst drunkards in the East End of London. My wife was a brokenhearted woman, and my children were as afraid of me as if I had been a wild beast. Today I have one of the happiest homes in London, and when I come home at the close of the day my wife and children are glad to see me. Jesus Christ has done this for me. This I know." [2]

The use of such a story justifies itself because it creates desires, renews purposes, intensifies the willingness to act, and transforms conduct. It brings the argument and thought into the spotlight and concentrates it in the hearer's imagination and often in his own living.

THE ART OF STORYTELLING

Like painting, storytelling is an art. There are a few persons highly gifted in the art. Many others learn its technique. But entirely too many go the way of unilluminated and dull speech largely because they either fail to give the work necessary to the learning or because they have never grasped the fact that even the poorest speaker can become an interesting illustrator if he tries hard enough.

There are certain principles which govern the use of the story and the preacher can learn to observe them. The man who is a "natural-born" storyteller uses them often without recognizing them as such, while the other man who may become as proficient learns by careful observation and practice. Study of the short story, its composition, its effectiveness, the reasons for its pungent vividness and centrality of effect

will yield valuable assistance. "The distinguishing factors of the short story are its brevity and its concentration in which concentration is paramount." The best advice is to avoid using irrelevant thoughts or words.

Outstanding Characteristics

There are four outstanding characteristics of a good story: (1) There is a beginning; (2) There must be action; (3) A climax is reached; (4) The conclusion ends it. These seem very simple, yet each is important in itself and demands careful attention.

The Introduction

Here is the real test of the storyteller's ability. In one or two brief sentences he must arouse curiosity, find a common interest, and launch his story. Usually the introduction should answer three simple questions: Who? When? and Where? It is not always necessary to include all of these. It is most important, however, that the congregation be intrigued by a carefully and skillfully worded introduction so that with natural interest and anticipation they will desire to follow the rest of the events.

The Action

There must follow action or a succession of events to carry the interest forward. The length of this and the variety of presentation, whether by conversation, picturesque description, or narration, will depend entirely upon the story to be

told, the purpose in the sermon, and the result desired. Paramount is the fact that all must lead to the climax. Every word and description must point to the moral choice or dilemma. There must be no inadvertence or casual remark which would divert attention.

Here is an illustration which, although of but three sentences, introduces the story in the first, moves it suggestively through the action, and quickly comes to a startling climax: "A minister visited one of his parishioners on a farm which, hitherto a failure, was now, by dint of tireless labor, being made a success. 'So,' said the minister, 'God and you are getting on very well here.' 'Yes,' said the farmer, 'but you should have seen this place before, when God was trying to handle it alone.'"

Dr. Fosdick brings its point clearly to attention as he adds: "Exactly! To start thus with a difficult situation as a place to begin being what Paul called a fellow-worker with God, is the very stuff of robust Christianity."[3]

A longer story involving several elements and covering some years is carried along in its action without the loss of interest as told by Dr. Gilkey:

"Thirty years ago the visiting preacher at an Eastern university took as his text one Sunday morning, 'I am the door.' He pictured life as a series of rooms leading one into the other: home to school, school to college, college out into active life; each room a preparation for the next. What then of life itself? His closing words no hearer could easily forget. Life itself, he said, seems to bring us at last only to a

blank wall. But there stands One saying down the generations, 'I am the door.'

"Twenty-five years later that same preacher's younger son had become one of the foremost medical scientists of his generation. In the mid-forties he was stricken with inoperable cancer, and his colleagues gave him six months to live. For eighteen months he looked death in the face with level eyes; and one of his medical associates has put into memorable words an experience shared during those months by many of his friends: 'The proof of a man's life—how much has been the living of a formula and how much an inward light— may often be found in the manner of his facing death. For courage is still, as it has always been, a thing of great beauty, that springs, whatever its form and expression, from an inner source of moral power. We wish, for ourselves and the ordinary human being, a swift and merciful death, which is most easily supported with dignity and composure. For him we would not have had it other than it came. Those who were fortunate in seeing him during those eighteen months when he and death sat face to face—who dreaded their first visits and came out gladly and inspired with a new faith in the nobility and courage to which rare men can attain—these know that the ugliness and cruelty of death were defeated. Death had no triumph, and he died as he had lived—with patience and love and submission in his heart, with the simple faith of a trustful child, and the superb gallantry of a great soul.'

"But even these words fail to convey the full measure of

his spiritual victory. Only a few weeks before his death, the doctor-son said to his preacher-father, speaking of the spirit of unity and serenity that pervaded the entire household, 'If you want to see what the Kingdom of God is like, come over to 12 Irving Street.' When his father told a friend of it, he added, 'Every time I come into contact with the clarity of his mind and the serenity of his spirit, I am reminded of that great saying in the New Testament, "Death hath no more dominion over him." ' " [4]

While there is a story here, it is more than that, it is life, moving on toward that consummation most devoutly to be wished—not death and escape, but spiritual victory over life and death. And yet this event or series could be told so poorly as to destroy the effect and the spiritual value. Here is not physical action, but action of the mind and soul launching into the Great Adventure.

Study Jesus and his mastery over words in beginning without wasting a thought, pushing with lightning rapidity through the events, fraught with continuous suspense, described without an ill-spent word, to the moral crisis, and then quickly ended. Too much cannot be said about saying as little as possible in the story.

In the following story of Jesus you will note that there is not the simplicity of treatment one finds in the direct account of the two houses built on sand and stone, but several considerations and introspections which seem at first to be beside the point. Yet if you eliminate any one of them, you destroy the story—and who would add any other conversation or action! The story is a unity with every point pressing forward toward the unexpected but forceful conclusion:

"And he said also unto the disciples, There was a certain rich man, who had a steward; and the same was accused unto him that he was wasting his goods. And he called him, and said unto him, What is this that I hear of thee? render the account of thy stewardship; for thou canst be no longer steward. And the steward said within himself, What shall I do, seeing that my lord taketh away the stewardship from me? I have not strength to dig; to beg I am ashamed. I am resolved what to do, that, when I am put out of the stewardship, they may receive me into their houses And calling to him each one of his lord's debtors, he said to the first, How much owest thou unto my lord? And he said, A hundred measures of oil. And he said unto him, Take thy bond, and sit down quickly and write fifty. Then said he to another, And how much owest thou? And he said, A hundred measures of wheat. He saith unto him, Take thy bond, and write fourscore. And his lord commended the unrighteous steward because he had done wisely: for the sons of this world are for their own generation wiser than the sons of light. And I say unto you, Make to yourselves friends by means of the mammon of unrighteousness: that, when it shall fail, they may receive you into the eternal tabernacles." [5]

The body of your story will need to move forward rapidly, maintaining the suspense, toward the crisis.

The Climax

It is at the climax that the story succeeds or fails. It matters not how well the interest is created at the beginning, nor how it is maintained through the events that foretell a struggle, if the issue never comes and the climax is never reached. Many a story dies "a-borning" because the preacher does not plan carefully the focal point of the action. A narration of events, which has no point, however interesting, is valueless.

The daily life of the people in a congregation is a succession of crises. The story which would be of value to them in the heat of the day must rise into increasing tension until quite suddenly it reaches the breaking point, and then is settled.

Everyone has heard someone tell a humorous story that was not funny at all; it simply trailed off, and the crowd laughed merely out of respect. We Americans in our self-conceit like to accuse the Englishman of being unable to appreciate a joke. One Englishman, it is said, was in a group and heard this riddle: "Why is a man's neck like a typewriter?" The answer came, "Because it is Underwood." The Englishman laughed with the crowd and thought it a capital joke. Later he said to a friend as follows: "Why is a man's neck like a typewriter?" When his friend could not answer, the Englishman replied, "Because it is like a Remington"—and never understood why his friend did not laugh.

How easy it is for all of us to tell a bootless story, to find we have lost the interest or just run out! The religious and moral story must have point. In the climax the right conclusion must be forthcoming and no one should be in doubt for a moment but that it is the right conclusion. It is as important that the climax be sudden or unpredictable as well as that it be satisfying. Failure here is dead failure for the entire story. The preacher should consider from every angle the climax to each story that its impression be indelible and memory-marked.

THE CONCLUSION

It is necessary for the story to end. Sometimes the climax is the end. If so, leave it there. Usually a few brief sentences are needed to relieve the tension and bring the congregation back to the world around them, and to enable them to feel the story a part of their own existence. The good story does not need comment. It only needs completion and resolution.

In the final story at the close of the Sermon on the Mount the climax is built up to a dramatic fashion: "A foolish man, who built his house upon the sand: and the rain descended, and the floods came, and the winds blew, and smote upon that house; *and it fell:*" (How powerful and final that climax! and then the conclusion, how satisfying:) "and great was the fall thereof." The story is left thus with its cataclysmic finish and without any running comment or moral to enforce or rather to weaken it.

THE PSYCHOLOGY OF ILLUSTRATING

I had played tennis for some years before reading and studying a chapter on "The Psychology of Tennis" in a book by big "Bill" Tilden, then world champion. It gave me mental assistance which enabled me to win many a close set and match that might otherwise have been lost. In brief, there are several points in both a game and a set which it is far more important to win than any other points. Winning these particular rallies gives a player a tremendous psychological advantage over his opponent. The odd points are more important than the even ones. The first point lends a feeling of achievement to the winner and a sense of failure to the loser, small perhaps but valuable. Of course knowing that winning the third point in a game or the third game of a set is of more value than either the second or fourth means little unless there has been an enormous amount of practice and thorough development of skill.

There is a certain psychology in the art of illustration which is serviceable when learned. In fact, it is necessary, but it cannot in any sense take the place of hard work in the building and use of illustrations. While a preacher may know the elements which make storytelling effective and be able to tell wherein a particular incident fails or succeeds, yet such knowledge will never be a substitute for constant attention to practical details and continued practice in building the illustration itself.

The secret of this psychology is similar to that of the short story. The narrative must come to *a climax as near to the end as possible*. Everything is to build directly into the crisis and as soon as this climax is reached, or as nearly thereafter as possible, the matter must end. Many persons ruin their stories by never coming to a height or, having reached the summit, trail endlessly on until the point is forgotten. It would be profitable to study the stories given throughout this text, as well as others found in sermons, to feel the force of this always-to-be-remembered rule—bring the illustration to a pointed climax; then end it quickly.

"Henry Van Dyke was standing on a hill back of the Belgian lines, and with Albert, King of the Belgians, was looking over the section overrun by the German army. Albert had been defeated, but planned some day to regain possession of the land and return in triumph to Brussels, the capital. Dr. Van Dyke asked him, 'What road does Your Majesty expect to take to Brussels?' The King replied, 'There are three possible roads. I plan to go straight ahead, and in spite of the opposition, to regain the capital. The road to the left leads down by the sea, where it is low and muddy; there we might be pushed back into the sea or find the going slow and difficult. The road to the right is over the hills, winding and tortuous. It is too long and we would be defeated. We cannot go these ways. So I have chosen the other.'"

This is a report of the conversation involving all the facts, but how inane compared to the following description of the scene and the climax as related by Dr. Ivan Lee Holt in the introduction to a sermon, "The Road Ahead":

"After a bitter fight in Belgium Henry Van Dyke, then United States minister to Holland, was standing on a hill back of the Belgian lines, looking toward Brussels and the section of the country overrun by the German Army. By his side stood Albert, King of the Belgians, brave in defeat and confident that one day the land would again be his kingdom. Asked Dr. Van Dyke, 'What road does Your Majesty expect to take to Brussels?' King Albert replied: 'There are three possible roads. This one on the left leads down by the sea. It is low and frequently muddy; there an army may be thrown into the sea, and if it escapes that fate it is very difficult to advance there. The road on the right leads over the hills, but it winds and turns; it is too long and it would be impossible to go that way. The third road leads straight ahead of us; down that we must go.' 'But, Your Majesty must remember that the enemy is strongly intrenched there,' was Dr. Van Dyke's comment. Quickly came Albert's answer: 'The enemy is there, but we will sweep him aside. One day I will ride in victory to our city, with my queen at my side and my loyal troops at my back.' " [6]

This must never be forgotten: The end! It is the epitome of the story! When you have finished, stop, but do it gracefully.

THE LENGTH OF THE STORY

There is always a certain limit to the modern sermon. Few preachers can use over twenty to thirty minutes and still keep the people coming. If the major portion of the sermon is given to substantial thought, it is apparent that a story of considerable length is impossible.

It seems to me there is a place for one who has attained

proficiency in this art to proclaim the divine message at a sermon hour by giving without comment a great story. Of course it would need to be, in both composition and delivery, everything that the word "great" implies. And yet if the preacher is able to create, as did Henry Van Dyke in *The Other Wise Man,* an occasional story to fit a season or important Christian experience, it would carry the message with reviving power.

But next to a story filling the preaching hour, it is possible to invent or find a story for a certain message which, although of some length, fits perfectly. There are occasions when for the sake of variety and effectiveness a preacher will choose this longer tale.

However, many stories are short enough, or can be abridged without adversely affecting their usefulness, so that they can be told in a comparatively small amount of time. It is sometimes possible to relate the principal value of a man's life in one or two sentences. It is profitable to study Dr. Fosdick's remarkable epitomes of different characters. Here are a few:

"We thought, perhaps, that a scientist like Pasteur, upon whose titanic work modern medicine rests, must have had lusty health to labor with. We discover that he had a paralytic stroke at forty-six and was handicapped for life. We thought, perhaps, that a man like Henry M. Stanley, acclaimed of the whole world and buried from Westminster Abbey, must have had a grand heritage. We find he was brought up in an almshouse, and that his real name was not

Stanley at all. We find Beethoven writing music although deaf and Milton writing poetry although blind, and we discover that in general the great work of the world has been done by handicapped people." [7]

We might take, for instance, Hawthorne's *The Great Stone Face,* which we use here as an example because it is so familiar. That story may be used in a sermon somewhat at length, introducing the various characters, each a concise photograph of a living counterpart. Or it could be abbreviated into several paragraphs. Dr. Roy L. Smith does this concisely as follows:

"Back among the beautiful White Mountains of New Hampshire is a most unusual rock formation which has been known for years as 'The Old Man of the Mountain.' It stands out against the sky, a perfect profile of a man's head, with a resemblance to the figure of an old pioneer with his coonskin cap that is almost uncanny. Years ago Nathaniel Hawthorne immortalized it in his story, *The Great Stone Face,* which is the tale of a boy who became great through keeping a great ideal before himself. Looking up at the face on the mountainside, the boy invested it with personality and strove, year after year, to imitate the virtues he believed his hero of the mountain to possess. Just as Ernest, in Hawthorne's story, reached the heights by keeping his eyes on the great stone face, so we may yet redeem life by lifting up our eyes unto the hills." [8]

Instead of the involved story, or the one abbreviated, we may condense it into several brief sentences. Rarely will a story which is written be suitable to a sermon without changing it to agree with the particular application and the time element.

IMAGINATIVE SELECTION

It is proper that we again bring to attention the matter of finding the proper story to suit the desired place in the sermon. This will depend upon the theme, upon the point at issue, upon the result expected in the mind, feelings, and action of the congregation.

Margaret Eggleston, one of the outstanding storytellers of our times, makes a pertinent suggestion: "If you hear a good story, jot down the outline. Then when you have reached your office or home, fill it in in your own words. In this way you will get many of your most effective stories. Not long ago a lady wrote asking me for the publisher of three stories that she had heard me tell. Two of those stories were built out of incidents I had seen when riding in her car with her by my side. The other I had heard told in a sermon in the church which we both attended." [9]

When you have chosen the theme to be illustrated, select the climax first. Usually any story can be turned into several crises, if properly handled and without prejudicing the facts. Find in your own mind the great moral crisis of the story. Bring that in mental picture, and probably in writing, to a central focus, stated as briefly and pointedly as possible. If this is done properly, the value of the story then can be effectively presented. Last, select the introduction and the conclusion. Ask yourself, "How can I introduce this with the greatest natural interest on the part of my congregation?" and when that is settled, ask yourself, "How can I conclude most effectively?"

If the preacher can fix in his own mind imaginatively the focal point, call it what you will, conflict, dilemma, crisis, climax; then introduce it interestingly, building the series of events up to this turning point; and finally can end his story briefly and with grace, he will have a powerful instrument to work his message into the hearts and lives of his people.

Getting Ready for the Pulpit

It would be puerile to analyze for a person about to eat a meal the actions which are necessary to that process. It seems equally so to outline the steps through which one needs to go in preparing the story for pulpit deliverance. And yet these following suggestions must be entered into, either separately and consciously, or in combination and more or less without deliberately intending such preparation. It is well for the preacher, having decided upon a particular illustration, to give considerable attention to it in private, alone.

Write down the story in full, if at all possible. This is the better by far since it leaves no doubts. The fleeting ideas and words are caged. How often all of us have had a splendid idea or the most fitting description, and, not writing it down, while our thoughts left the room, the priceless bird flew out the window, never to return. When an illustration is written down, it can never escape.

If you do not write it on paper, do so the more arduous

way—on the tablet of your mind. But be sure it is written there plainly, in detail.

Having written, either on paper or in the mind, then enter imaginatively and realistically into the scene. If the story is not presented in a vital fashion, it loses largely its usefulness. The preacher in his study can analyze all the elements of the story, word and reword them properly, enter into them meditatively and imaginatively, until he has become possessed by the realities behind the narrative.

Bible scenes are two thousand and more years old, and if people today see them as more than a recital of historical events they already know or don't care about, it will be because imagination has touched them with living fire. Dr. Jowett advises young preachers to cultivate assiduously the historical imagination so that the life of old becomes vividly alive in the present year of our Lord. A necessary prerogative is the ability of the preacher to re-enter the ancient day or the characters of the persons, to live with and in these other times and people until he sees and feels as they do.

However, imagination must be responsible to truth, controlled by facts. Some preachers have a way of delineating Jesus in a way no word or syllable of the New Testament would justify. Undisciplined imagination is like a child without restraint. "The imagination finds its leaping ground from the solid plane of knowledge." [10] True imagination in contrast to a weak watery illustration founded upon fantasy is based upon sure insight, clear judgment, and abiding faith in God.

Such reliving of the scenes requires solitariness and meditation.

RECITE ALOUD

Having written and imaginatively entered character and situation, it is profitable to tell the story aloud, or at least verbally in the mind exactly as the preacher anticipates giving it. Often he will discover that it does not sound as he intends, that adjustments are necessary, that the climax needs to be reworded or slightly changed in emphasis. Occasionally this practice will be invaluable—for discovery before delivery is far better than regret after.

Under the old psychology a personality was divided into reason, will, and emotion. Later it was discovered that you could not take a boy and chop off his reason from his feeling or his volition, and still have a boy. He was a personality, a unity, co-ordinating his whole action, and divisible only in the mind of the analyst. The three steps outlined above, writing, imaginatively relieving the events, and speaking mentally or aloud are all parts of the same process. It is possible for them to be distinct and separate, but in all probability they will be woven into a unitary procedure. Creative imagination will dictate the writing and wording, as it projects the story to the congregation as the preacher expects it to be next Sunday. While the picture delineates itself, writing will take place, the effect upon the people all the while evaluating the procedure, until, out of meditation and study, the final story or illustration emerges, akin both to the event and to the particular audience who shall hear it.

POETRY

Very closely resembling and probably a part of the story method of preaching is the use of poetry in the sermon. Its value, which is probably far in excess of what any of us can determine, has already been discussed. The fact that some person asks you who wrote a certain verse you quoted or where he might find it, or that someone else testifies to the uplift of a poem is only a minor indication of the worth. Far more significant is the quickening interest of any congregation, educated or uneducated, privileged or without advantages, in city or country, when a poem, well-told, is brought into the message. The beauty of holiness can be expressed in verse as no prose can ever describe it. The poet epitomizes wisdom in rhythm that sings its way into the soul. Poetry grips the emotions and creates new attitudes and purposes. Life is renewed and the City of God made real by the inspired vision of the poet.

READ THE POEM?

There are certain principles of conduct which a preacher will follow if poetry is to find its greatest usefulness to him. The first and unbreakable law is: Never Read! That is, unless you want to discount your effort at least fifty per cent. I have heard many men try it and never, with only one exception, has it been successful. I am sure that in this instance it would have been at least as effective had there been no paper between the man and his people.

I heard a bishop deliver an address on missions which lifted the entire audience to new heights and made them akin to the world as Christian brethren. He had a notebook on the pulpit near by to which he had not referred during the address. But as he closed, he reached over, picked up the notebook, and read a poem which should have been a fitting climax to such a noble message. As he read I watched the congregation disintegrate, lose interest, and become restless for him to finish. Far better had he never used that poem, as suitable as it was, than to have ruined his message by such an unnecessary desecration. I vowed then that unless I was willing to give the time required to memorize a poem, I would not be guilty of such a scene as I beheld, and which I, too, had often done before.

It is not necessary to read. It takes no genius to memorize. Psychology has proved by innumerable tests, and one's own trials will determine as well, that any normal person of average intelligence, of whatever age, can learn to memorize.

How to Memorize Poetry

There are a few simple aids which will enable a man to fasten a verse or more in his mind in the least amount of time. They are familiar to everyone who has studied the learning process.

First, memorize the poem as a whole. Never try a verse or a few lines, adding other verses or lines. This is fatal because not only does it take longer to learn in this manner, but also the mind, as one recites the poem in public, will hesitate and often stop at the end of each separate part memorized. It will fail to catch hold of the next line immediately. Disaster follows.

Read the entire poem, no matter how long the part you wish to use. Read it completely through again and again, studying the meaning and enveloping yourself in the thought. After some time the poem will seem suddenly to pop up into consciousness. If there are submerged lines or a verse which is not retained well enough, then it is time to go over that section to fix it in the mind.

Second, it is better to take a week to learn a poem, giving a few minutes two or three times a day, than to attempt to learn it all at one or two sittings. Psychologists have proved that the learning process goes on in the intermissions as well as at the time of intense concentration.

Third, the best time of day is just before retiring. It seems as though the mind will absorb and unify the work of a few conscious moments just before sleep into a subsconscious retention of the material. The mind will go on working while the body rests, until upon waking, many a morning, a single reading of the poem will finally fix the result.

Fourth, a poem memorized and ready for use today will soon slip back into the subsconscious where it will remain, just out of reach. If it is desired to use that poem again, it will require re-learning. That can be done, however, in only a fraction of the time necessary for the first memorization. The chances are that it will be then a permanent conscious possession.

A Vocabulary of Poetry

The prime difficulty which the preacher faces in the preparation of his sermon is the lack of poems at his finger tips when he most wants them. He comes to a place in his sermon where a verse would suit admirably, give it the bright-winged flight. He recognizes the need, but does not know where to find the right poem. Or he may have arrived at a point at which a certain poem would be most apt, but he is ignorant of that poem's existence, and the sermon must go its lone way unblessed. No one can tell how much our sermons have suffered from unfamiliarity and lack of experience on the part of the preacher with the rich storehouses of poetry. In his famine he does not know that the warehouses of Joseph in Egypt are full of harvested grain.

There is a way, however, by which a preacher may make available those resources for his sermons. In his devotional hours he may well give time to familiarizing himself with the library of the best inspirational poetry. For the sake of his own soul he may read the literature of religious verse. Saturating himself in these wellsprings of distilled experiences, he will be able to speak from the deepened appreciation of the most worthwhile in life. If he becomes thoroughly familiar with the world's great religious poetry, he will also be able to know where to find a poem expressing a certain theme suitable in the sermon he is preparing.

There is yet a better way in which he will create a vocabulary of poetry to serve his commands. If he sets out with some such book as *Quotable Poems* [11] and attempts to memorize at least one or even two poems each week, whether he requires them for his sermons at hand or not, he will in some months or a year or two have an abundant store. For the minister whose sole concern is the sermon due next Sunday morning and another in the evening, this may seem far-stretching. But for the man who desires to deliver himself at his best for the Kingdom's sake ten years from now, it will not be without ample and abiding rewards.

This may seem difficult at first, but it is entirely within reach. The process of learning suggested above makes attainable the memorization of two poems of average length each week.

The strange fact, if it is unusual, is that after a month or two of practice it will take not much more than half as long to master a poem. The other interesting discovery will be that in the dire necessity of some sermon preparation, there will flash an image, a line, or a subject from some poem which is so completely apropos as to make well worth while all effort and study. It was but a labor of joy.

Poems so learned cannot be kept at the forefront of consciousness. They will slip into the subconscious, where they will be only partially available. And yet it will be surprising how some suggestion will come to the surface when least expected as though in answer to the touch of some Aladdin's lamp. When that happens, it will be little or no task to go back to the poem in book or file and re-memorize it in its entirety—or that section desired for the immediate illumination.

240

The preacher who will apply himself assiduously to the study and memorizing of poetry will find after a few years that he has built a treasurehouse of inspiration and has added appreciably to the effectiveness of his ministry. Far more, he has been putting into his people forces, alike unto heaven's own music, which have been lifting them to higher planes of living, "who walk through this life as though keeping step with music heard from far above it."

THE ART OF EFFECTIVE
PRESENTATION

THE man in the pulpit in his own person enlightens or obscures his teaching. His personal appearance, his bearing, his action, gestures, and mannerisms affect decidedly the attractiveness and appeal of his sermon. Probably more often than we as preachers realize some point which should have driven its way home we blunt by some mannerism, grotesque gesture, or the lowering of the eyes to a manuscript.

The action of the man in the pulipt begins long before he appears in front of the congregation. It is dependent upon whether he has lived the past days, and years as well, in the Presence, from Whom all spiritual life flows. It is dependent also upon the intensity of preparation and the methods he has used. When one is already in the pulpit in the act of preaching, it is too late to measure and weigh the effect of certain practices or to experiment in the conduct of one's self. This must be accomplished in thought during the preceding days.

It is during the hours in the study and in the decision a

man makes as to his method of presentation which determines at least to fair degree his effectiveness on Sunday.

Basic is the method of preparation. Though it takes place apart and separate from the people, it leads directly to them in the Sunday service. The use the preacher has made of the hours in the study enables them to see clearly or with difficulty. There are three well-known and practiced methods, each with its defects as well as its virtues, each used by innumerable men. Every preacher must choose for himself the method which best is adapted to his temperament, his abilities, and the congregations he anticipates serving.

The Written Sermon

There are certain distinct advantages to writing the sermon out in full. The thought can be arranged in perfect sequence, the illustrations carefully selected and placed, and the entire composition phrased in the best possible language. The advantages are so great that it seems to me that, at least for the first ten years or more of a man's ministry, if not always, he should write in full at least one sermon each week. There are many ministers in busy pastorates, some with hundreds of members to care for, who have the regular habit of developing and writing two sermons each week. The labor is great, but the results, cumulative through the years, are well worth every effort.

Canon Harold A. Prichard lists nine prominent and powerful preachers, giving their testimony about their own preaching.[1] Eight out of nine write their sermons in full. Bishop

Edwin Holt Hughes told a group of ministers, "Whatever power I have had in preaching, I attribute in no small way to the fact that I have spent a lifetime writing my sermons."

The efficacy of such discipline so far as illustrations go is immediately apparent. It is easy for the preacher to appraise his written manuscript: Are there too many or not enough illustrations? Do they clarify or are they unnecessary? Is there variety? Are they properly developed so as to produce the desired effect, climax, vividness? Is the language clear, precise, and illuminative as well? Will they tend to move out of the sermon into the lives of the people? Analysis of one's manuscript will reveal what no amount of mental juggling will do with the unwritten sermon.

Reading from Manuscript

However, when the preacher decides what he will do with that manuscript, his fate is written. When he takes it into the pulpit to read from it—unless he is one of a small class of geniuses—he immediately obscures some of its meaning. He may read well; he may discourse learnedly or in well-rounded phrases not possible in extempore speaking; but he has not preached as he might without it. There is the inevitable barrier between the preacher and the congregation. They feel subtly that the preacher is not adjusting himself to them, to the thought transpiring in their minds. They also know that he is doing no thinking—that was done long ago; he is simply reading a past production. Vitality and glowing creativeness are gone.

I have often been in an audience when the speaker brought forth his manuscript. Invariably, without a single exception, one could see the congregation sag, the attention diverted, the interest lessen. Few men have been able to overcome such a handicap. Recently I sat in a great gathering as one of the bishops delivered an address. At the conclusion a friend sitting next wrote on his program: "He read it. He read it poorly. With exceptions, it was not worth reading."

In spite of the statement of Dr. Bernard Iddings Bell, himself a preacher of note but who composes as he says only four or five sermons a year, that "a reasonable amount of practice will enable anybody to read a sermon as freely as he preaches extemporaneously,"[2] there is hardly a parish minister anywhere who can read without depreciating the effectiveness of his delivery. Manuscript preaching is a late development in the Christian Church, unknown in the early centuries, and it is one instance in which modernity is no improvement. If the best you can do is read from a written manuscript, try with all earnestness to make it as unobtrusive as possible. But do not yield to this method finally until you have earnestly attempted another way.

PREACHING FROM NOTES

The second method is to preach from an outline or notes. Two types of preparation can be used—namely, to write the sermon in full, after which an outline is made in more or less completeness, or to prepare the sermon in outline form only. We are viewing the sermon now from the effect upon the congregation as it is preached from the pulpit. Let the preacher choose the kind of preparation he shall give, knowing that in the long run the thoroughly written manuscript will yield larger dividends.

It is apparent that the preacher who uses an outline will have larger freedom than the man with his manuscript. If the preparation has been thorough, practically every advantage of the written paper will continue under this method. Often the very words of the manuscript will be repeated as they are written. Any change the preacher feels called to make in the moment's inspiration can be brought in as though it were a part of an unbroken cloth.

Illustrations, particularly, will have a freedom and dynamic which will appeal to the listeners. There will be freshness and animation of rare value. Out of the nine eminent preachers quoted by Dr. Prichard, eight of whom had written the sermon in full, only one reads from the manuscript. The others use notes or preach without any paper before them.

Without Crutches

An experience of my own, which may be of little value to others, has been of inestimable value to me. I had always preached from an outline, having preceded that, in almost every instance for several years, with writing in full both Sunday sermons. After dinner on this particular Sunday noon my wife asked, "How many times do you think you looked at your notes during the sermon?" "Not very often, I am sure," I confidently replied, "I knew that sermon better than usual." "You looked down at them forty-seven times in less than thirty minutes. I counted them." Then she added, "And for a man as tall as you are, you lose the congregation's attention each time."

I resolved then and there that I would go into the pulpit next Sunday without any notes whatsoever and that, sink or swim, succeed or fail, I'd never use them again. I never have; and I believe the increased effectiveness has been most rewarding.

EXTEMPORE PREACHING

That leads us to the third method used by many preachers, to give the sermon without manuscript or notes of any kind. The preacher thus provides a passport by which the congregation may enter his soul. Nothing now hinders; there is no barrier between the thought of the minister and the moving thought of the people.

There is, of course, the danger of forgetting; but with careful preparation this can be overcome. And it is true that once in a while some item is left out, even a good illustration. But the benefits so overwhelmingly make up for such slight lapses. And again, the fear most of us have that memory will fail is altogether unwarranted. Few, if any, of us ever trust our memory enough. It will prove as faithful a servant as we have faith that it will be. It is surprising how an outline or even the entire written sermon appears before the mind if it is given a chance. Practice enables a person in an incredibly short time mentally to photograph the outline, especially if one meditates upon his message in the presence of God, prayerfully and with dependence upon the Spirit for direction.

It is possible that this method, which by far is the better, cannot be used by all ministers. But it is well worth trying. Use the method which best suits your own temperament and abilities, remembering that so far as illustrations are concerned, the less you depend upon that which is written the better.

It is a certainty that rare is the person who can read an illustration and make it seem real. Scarcer still is one who can read a story as well as with practice he could tell it. And it is almost impossible to find one who can make a poem come to life from a paper. However much you are forced to carry with you into the pulpit a detailed manuscript or outline of your thoughts, leave the paper when you come to your illustrations. Tell them simply and without affectation.

It is necessary to remind ourselves that there are a few preachers who, like George Whitefield, never write down on paper any ideas or sequence, but who preach like fire from high heaven. While every advantage of unrestrained liberty is theirs, they must be men who are rigorous enough in their thinking and honest enough in their mental application to forego the temptation to lax and loose preparation or speech. A man such as these is a genius who is beyond rules and regulations—and has ceased reading this discussion long ago.

In the Pulpit

At a meeting of the bishop and presiding elders during an Annual Conference session, a certain church was being considered. It was an unusual opportunity, but an exceedingly difficult field. It demanded extraordinary ability, abundance of energy, and acceptable preaching. No man with experience could be spared from as needy places elsewhere.

During the previous year the presiding elder of the district observed a young man, only a short time in the ministry, stationed on a small, scattered circuit. He had given evidence of ability and effectiveness so far as the limitations of the small field offered. Here was a man who had the possibilities of serving acceptably. The appointment would have to be made in faith that Peter would become the Rock.

It was not easy to make the selection, for it meant advancing a young man with little practical experience to twice his former salary—but more, to five times the responsibility. Could he do it acceptably? With the facts in mind, there was only one way of certainty, to make or refuse to make the appointment. The bishop and his associates had to take action. They made the assignment and the young man has proved by his achievements worthy of the faith placed in him.

Suppose that after the appointment the young minister had failed to deliver himself! Then the Cause which he represented would have suffered greatly.

The same situation faces the preacher in his sermons. Here he has a difficult and dark place in the sermon for next week, of strategic importance, which needs the helping service of a strong illustration. Searching he finally discovers what appears from all tests to be the promised assistant. But that is not enough! He must act, put the illustration into its position, not on paper or in the mind, but in the actual act of preaching.

However good the illustration appeared to be, suppose the preacher does not present it clearly and well! What matters it if he has ranged the world for illuminations, has found many of value, has kept them well-docketed, has placed this excellent one into his manuscript, and then fails in the delivery! No matter how fine an illustration may be, its whole usefulness depends upon whether the minister has presented it with clarity and force so that the congregation is affected and changed by it.

The key to everything about illustrating sermons is here —the delivery!

It is when the man of God is in the pulpit before his congregation that the sermon becomes "truth through personality." The final product will depend upon the sermon having been begun early enough, at least a week before, having been worked upon assiduously and faithfully, having been immersed in the thought and prayer of the preacher as he lives the truth in the presence of God, and then in the church service itself having been poured out as an animated part of the man's own personality. The preacher in the pulpit becomes a portal into heaven.

"The Reverend Thomas Binney of the King's Weigh House Chapel in London used to tell preachers that all that was necessary was to gather your materials and then set fire to them in the pulpit." [3]

THE SOUL OF THE BUILDER

Hᴇ is the best preacher I know," said one of four intimate friends concerning the late Dr. S. Parkes Cadman.

"He is a better pastor than he is a preacher," replied another.

"He is a better friend than either."

"I think," said the fourth, "that he is all that you have said. But he is more. If I were going to sum him up in a sentence, I would say that he is intensely human and intensely Christian."

In this description of one of our generation's best-loved ministers, is a Jacob's ladder of great preaching that leads from earth to heaven. At the bottom is a deep and abiding personal experience of Christ which ascends on steps of friendship with people of all conditions and degrees of life, through intimate and complete pastoral service to the acme of inspired preaching.

But let no one believe that Dr. Cadman did not labor prodigiously on his sermons. "I write all my sermons in full and then make careful notes of the manuscript," he states.[1]

So it is with all the men who preach at their best. They labor constantly at their task, trying to make their efforts as nearly perfect as possible. A recent article concerning Dr. Edgar De Witt Jones has this to say: "Intellectually Doctor Jones walks with kings, but he has never lost the common touch. . . . Love of his fellow man and a deep understanding are as grimly imbedded in his character as love of God. . . . He is scrupulous about the proper preparation of his sermons. Although one of the most brilliant and effective pulpit orators, a man whose splendid voice, perfect diction, faultless delivery, and deep scholarship might seem to fit him ideally for extemporaneous talk, he never depends on it. He believes that every preacher owes it to his congregation to be soundly prepared." [2]

He who would succeed should cultivate the artistic, the best sermon preparation in order to have the finest results. But after he has given his best effort in preparation he should not depend upon it alone, but also have a devotion to the people and a personal Christian experience.

Prepare in Advance

Sundays wait for no preacher, and sermon preparation must be carried on regularly and with fidelity. If other parish work has been allowed to take too much time, preaching suffers; and more, the people and the Kingdom suffer.

Those sermons worked on for weeks or months call out the best of illustrative material. Dr. F. S. Hickman once said that he had written fifty pages for one thirty-minute sermon.

The analogy of this book, like most analogies, breaks down somewhere. It is valuable up to a certain point. And let that place of weakness be pointed out here. While windows are manufactured products, real sermons are growths like flowers. They are not mechanical, but are vital, growing, living, spiritual realities. Out of the life of the preacher, nurtured in Christ Jesus, comes the message which develops into the final presentation. As the sermon idea expands illustrations grow into the living body of the sermon.

ELOQUENCE OF SOUL

Primary among the requisites of the preacher is an awakened imagination, which sees that every human being and every human relation has a place in God's beneficence. To picture the downtrodden, the disfranchised, the accused, the criminal, and the place under God they can and should occupy, is enough to stimulate the finest preaching. If the minister will seek to see as God sees, and formulate his conceptions in the best style, allowing the flame to burn as he speaks, his sermon will find its mark. There is a direct relation between eloquence in words and eloquence of soul. It is in the mystic symphony of God, the preacher's silent and meditative waiting, and the expectant congregation that divinity is mediated to man.

"I walk down the Valley of Silence—
Down the dim, voiceless valley, alone!

253

And I hear not the fall of a footstep
　　Around me, save God's and my own;
And the hush of my heart is as holy
　　As hovers where angels have flown!

In the hush of the Valley of Silence
　　I dream all the songs that I sing;
And the music floats down the dim Valley,
　　Till each finds a word for a wing,
That to hearts, like the Dove of the Deluge,
　　A message of Peace they may bring." [3]

Through inward vision the preacher must have the power to realize God. Through outward words he must have power of transmitting that vision to the congregation.

A SUBTLE DANGER

There is a subtle and costly temptation for any preacher with ability to tell incidents well, to picture Bible scenes capably, and to enthrall audiences with his diction. This is to substitute the superficial for depth, analysis, and close thinking.

In painting there are certain artists who subordinate structure and design to light and color. They sacrifice all the other elements of painting in order to capture the vivid and immediate impression. Kenyon Cox compares two hermits, one painted by Titian and the other by Sargent:

"The conception of Titian's St. Jerome in the Desert is perhaps more humanistic than religious. The figure of the saint on which everything converges is not merely robust, it is even a bit robustious. The picture affirms in its every detail the superior importance of man and his purposes to his natural environment. On the other hand, the impressionistic and pantheistic hermit of Sargent is almost entirely merged in the landscape; he is little more than a pretext for a study of the accidents of light. So far as their inner life is concerned the two hermits are plainly moving in opposite directions." [4]

Likewise, certain preachers use their gift at picturization to cover the canvas of their sermons with light and color, but do not regard certain standards of proportion. They are often known as "good storytellers," but the points of their stories are smothered in mere words, and are too soon forgotten. They are sometimes referred to as "good entertainers," as though the high calling of God's ministers were that of the buffoon.

How different with Christ! Can anyone forget the graphic recounting of the prodigal son, was there ever a more realistic balance of light and color, of day and night, life and death? And yet it is constrained by the law and order of the moral universe, the whole regulative system of God's supreme purpose. No man would ever accuse Jesus of telling a story for its own sake, or merely to add zest of color. The more intently one studies the figures of Jesus, the more one is impressed with the fact that through it all runs one increasing purpose. When one reads or hears some parable of Jesus like the one of the prodigal son, he forgets the story and says to himself, "There am I," or "I know someone like that."

No Substitutes

There can be no substitute for the spirit of the preacher, or his grasp of his message. No technique can replace earnestness and devotion to the living Word. Technically correct structure and well-formed stories will be no more than sounding brass or noisy cymbal without a fervent life filled with Christ.

Yet technique is necessary to project the message into the lives of the people. Recently I visited the Bureau of Investigation in Washington. Everywhere was evidence of accuracy, skill, persistence, supported by training in legal matters and in criminal detection. The men were expert in every detail: They qualified as public accountants; they used the most accurate methods of chemistry and photography; and their purpose was to track down crime. Such men put ministers to shame! With the purpose of remaking the world nearer to God's desire, we too often fail because we have not qualified to use the best of the speaker's art. There are few if any ministers who have reached such perfection that they cannot improve their preaching methods, their use of illustration, and their delivery. Fortunately, continuous practice and careful preparation will produce results.

The Highest Reality

The preacher is a storyteller. However, he should not be a teller of mere meaningless fables, but should clothe his truth with pointed incident to capture the highest reality. He is not a storyteller for entertainment, but one who, through imagination and high emotion, creates new life for his listeners. "Picturesqueness, dramatic art, contemporary illustrations, irony, humor, personal anecdotes, exaggerated emphasis, all have their place in preaching to ordinary people; but the aim of the sermon, the end of the effort must always be spiritual, lofty, tender, human, with more of the breath of Galilee than of Hollywood about it." [5]

The responsibility of the preacher is not to produce an artistic masterpiece called a sermon, nor to deliver a finished product and be satisfied that he has spoken truth in an excellent manner. Rather it is that the hearer perceives the truth and proceeds to act upon it. A deliverance is a sermon when it results in Christlike action.

"It was a successful operation," said the doctor, "but the patient died." A sermon may be technically correct, the procedure proper, the execution according to the rules, but the people may perish.

"The art of the preacher does not consist in making sentences or literature or constructing a sermon according to a perfect model. His art consists in so using his material that it will convey Spirit to the spirit of the other man. . . . The art of preaching is to transmit spirit and influence spirit by means of *words*." [6]

The artist-preacher must translate the words he finds in doctrines, creeds, dogmas, and the Bible, into his own experience and then interpret them in words of his own choosing that his hearers may weave them into their living experiences.

A Difficult Undertaking

It certainly should be understood by ministers, although many seem to overlook it, that creating a spiritual attitude, a response to other-than-human elements, developing moral conduct, is a most difficult task. One may talk endlessly and make no impression on the conduct of the people. He may preach upon a certain mode of action, say forgiveness, with frequent recurrence for months and yet find his people as stubborn as ever in their unrelenting attitudes toward each other.

Many modern ministers seem not to appreciate that mere knowledge is not wisdom, nor facts a guarantee of good conduct. Your people can have all knowledge and intellectual grasp and yet use it complacently for selfish, malicious, and hurtful purposes, with few qualms of conscience as to their actions.

Something vastly more than information and discussion and forum tactics is necessary. There must be a flowing of personality, God-filled, from the preacher to the people. Information must be given, perceived, appropriated, enveloped in character, filled with purpose, and translated into action. Mere discussions of war, alcohol, economic distress, personal despairs are not enough. There must come from the preacher to the people great convictions, life-and-death determinations, personal commitments which will risk everything for the desired end. "For to me to live is Christ" must be transmitted as electric waves through the speaker to those who hear.

THE SOUL OF THE BUILDER

We do not know enough about psychological processes, about spiritual awakening, about the genesis of the religious life in a person, about the hows and whys of a person's inward growth ever to say that, if such and such were done or said, certain predictable results would be accomplished. We do not have the precision of instruments or clinical information as has the doctor to prophesy that such a method of presentation of religious truth will yield a desired result.

However, certain practices through the ages upon the part of preachers has produced definite character and action. Experience has proved that illustrations, if rightly used, do lead people into Christian living. The Spirit of God does work through illuminations to quicken the imagination and direct the will. The speaker may not know when or how it occurs; he may catch it by the moistening of an eye, a softening of the expression, or never know it happened. But he does know that, somehow, through illustrations which light up the inner recesses of dormant powers, hopes, aspirations, and character achievements, the course of a human life is changed, for an hour or perhaps for eternity.

It would be most valuable if it could be ascertained the exact changes which have taken place in human personality during preaching, the precise moment in the discourse when the changes were stimulated, and the key to the stimulation. Probably more than all else it was the spirit-filled personality of the preacher. But undoubtedly it has been largely accomplished through the years by enkindling illustrations, living experiences, throbbing human incidents.

A Glorious Opportunity

While the preaching of a sermon to produce Christlike conduct is difficult, it is also the greatest opportunity ever presented to man. No one else ever has a finer chance than that permitted the preacher, as on a Sunday he stands before a congregation to mediate the Word of God. Then all his prior effort to find the proper and suitable illustration, his art in using it effectively, will serve to fulfill his calling as a representative of Jesus Christ. To work with God in the building of a new, a Christian world is his high privilege.

> "Creation's Lord, we give Thee thanks
>   That this our world is incomplete,
> That battle calls our marshaled ranks,
>   That work awaits our hands and feet,
> That Thou hast not yet finished man,
>   That we are in the making still—
> As friends who share the Maker's plan,
>   As sons who know the Father's will." [7]

REFERENCES AND NOTES

INTRODUCTION

1. Dowling, *The Power of Illustration,* page 24. (Colby and Co., 1848.)

2. John A. Kern, *The Ministry to the Congregation,* Chaps. 9 and 10. (Cokesbury Press.)

Chapter I

PREACHING IN WHICH PEOPLE SEE

1. Ruskin: *Modern Painters,* Vol. III, Pt. iv, Chap. xvi, par. 28.

2. Harold Adye Prichard: *The Minister, the Method, and the Message,* page 155.

3. Anne Shannon Monroe, "Seeing Out," in *Good Housekeeping,* February, 1936. Miss Monroe is the author of *Singing in the Rain,* etc.

Chapter II

THE MASTER STORYTELLER

1. A. E. Garvie, *The Christian Preacher,* pages 159, 160. (Scribners, 1921.)

2. *Ibid.,* page 150.

3. *Ibid.,* page 248.

4. *Ibid.,* page 250.

5. *Ibid.,* page 252.

6. *Ibid.,* page 254.

7. *Ibid.*, page 260.

8. George Buttrick, *The Parables of Jesus,* page 194. (Smith, 1928.) This is by far the most illuminating book on the parables, and to it I am greatly indebted. See also Halford E. Luccock, *Studies in the Parables of Jesus,* for interesting insights.

9. Matthew 10 : 19.

10. Matthew 18 : 9.

11. Matthew 21 : 33-41.

12. Matthew 21 : 42, 43, quoting Psalm 118 : 22 f.

13. William Wordsworth.

14. George Buttrick, *The Parables of Jesus,* page xxi. (Smith, 1928.)

15. Edwin Markham, "Earth Is Enough."

16. George Buttrick, *The Parables of Jesus,* page xxi. (Smith, 1928.)

17. Matthew 13 : 15, quoting Isaiah 6 : 9, 10.

18. Matthew 21 : 45.

19. Matthew 21 : 28-34.

CHAPTER III

VARIETIES OF ILLUSTRATIONS AND THEIR USE

1. Louise Owen, *Poems of Enjoyment,* page 217.

2. Matthew 12 : 32.

3. Matthew 12 : 36, 37.

4. Luke 15 : 3-7.

5. Matthew 5 : 13, 14 and 6 : 22.

6. Quoted by George Buttrick, *The Parables of Jesus.* (Smith, 1928.)

7. Author unknown.

8. Charles Gilkey, *Perspectives,* page 6. (Harpers, 1933.)

REFERENCES AND NOTES

9. Harry Emerson Fosdick, *The Hope of the World,* page 138.

10. George Buttrick, "Why the Church," a sermon in the *Christian Century Pulpit,* December, 1932.

11. These selections from the *Reader's Digest* are from the following: Enid Bagnold, B. M. Bower, Thomas Hardy, Kate O'Brien, Margaret Pedler, Frank Norris, "Overheard," and the last, Unknown.

12. The title of the first sermon in a book by the same name, Allan Knight Chalmers.

13. Edgar De Witt Jones, "Blundering into Paradise."

14. J. W. G. Ward, *The Refiner's Fire,* page 23.

15. Charles Gilkey, *Perspectives.* (Harpers, 1933.)

16. M. S. Rice, *Hearing the Unheard.* (Harpers, 1933.)

17. Roy L. Smith, *Suburban Christians.* (Harpers, 1933.)

18. Charles R. Brown, *Finding Ourselves.* (Harpers, 1935.)

19. Walter Russell Bowie, *When Christ Passes By.*

20. R. H. Daugherty.

21. Ralph Sockman, *The Unemployed Carpenter.* (Harpers, 1933.)

22. John H. Lathrop, *Toward Discovering Religion.*

23. John Haynes Holmes, *The Sensible Man's View of Religion.*

24. Edgar De Witt Jones, "Blundering into Paradise."

25. T. C. Speers, *The Power of the Commonplace.*

26. Paul W. Quillian.

27. Miles H. Krumbine, *Little Evils That Lay Waste Life.*

28. Frederick F. Shannon, *The Land of Beginning Again.*

29. Frederick B. Fisher, *Can I Know God?* (Harpers, 1934.)

30. H. A. Overstreet, *Influencing Human Behavior*, pages 12, 13.

31. Charles R. Brown, *Finding Ourselves*, pages 123-125. (Harpers, 1935.)

32. *Ibid.*, pages 88, 89.

33. Harry Emerson Fosdick, sermon on "The Ghost of a Chance," in *The Power to See It Through*, page 93. (Harpers, 1935.)

34. M. S. Rice, *Hearing the Unheard*, page 3. (Harpers, 1935.)

35. From *Facing Life with Jesus Christ*, page 83. (Board of Christian Education, Methodist Episcopal Church, South.)

36. Dowling, *The Power of Illustration*, page 43.

37. M. S. Rice, *Hearing the Unheard*, page 23. (Harpers, 1935.)

38. Arthur John Gossip, *The Hero in Thy Soul*, page 91. (Scribners, 1936.)

39. Author unknown.

40. Grace Noll Crowell, "Light of the Years." (Harpers.)

41. *Ibid.*

42. Sermon by the author in *Christian Century Pulpit*, February, 1933.

43. Robert Browning.

44. Richard Lovelace.

45. John Timothy Stone, in the *Christian Century Pulpit*, October, 1934, page 230.

46. Ella Wheeler Wilcox, "Progress," from *Quotable Poems*, Clark and Gillespie.

REFERENCES AND NOTES

CHAPTER IV

GATHERING MATERIALS—EXPERIENCE AND OBSERVATION AS A SOURCE

1. McComb, *Preaching in Theory and Practice*, page 17.

2. Edgar De Witt Jones, *American Preachers of Today*, page 29. (Bobbs-Merrill, 1933.)

3. Carl S. Patton, *The Use of the Bible in Preaching*, page 112. (Willett, Clark and Co., 1936.)

4. S. Parkes Cadman, *Ambassadors of God*, page 251. (By permission of the Macmillan Company, publishers.)

5. Charles R. Brown, *Finding Ourselves*, page 87. (Harpers, 1935.)

6. Mark 4: 26-29.

7. Carl S. Patton, *The Use of the Bible in Preaching*, page 244. (Willett, 1936.)

8. Ralph W. Sockman, *The Unemployed Carpenter*, page 32, sermon subject, "Bridges Not Burned." (Harpers, 1933.)

9. Carl S. Patton, *The Use of the Bible in Preaching*, page 129. (Willett, 1936.)

10. Lynn Harold Hough, *The University of Experience*, page 6. (Harpers, 1933.)

11. William H. Carruth, "Each in His Own Tongue."

12. Charles R. Brown, *Finding Ourselves*, pages 22, 23, sermon, "How Shall We Think About God?" (Harpers, 1935.)

13. Charles W. Gilkey, *Perspectives*, page 22. (Harpers, 1933.)

14. Halford E. Luccock, *Preaching Values in New Translations of the New Testament*, page 185. (Copyright, 1928. By permission of Abingdon Press.)

15. Halford E. Luccock, *Preaching Values in the Old Testament,* page 84. (Abingdon, 1933.)

16. Halford E. Luccock, *Preaching Values in New Translations of the New Testament,* page 124. (Abingdon, 1928.)

17. Halford E. Luccock, *Preaching Values in the Old Testament,* page 19. (Abingdon, 1933.)

18. John A. Kern, *The Ministry to the Congregation,* page 220. (Cokesbury Press.)

19. Article in *The Christian Herald,* September, 1936.

20. Article in *The Christian Century,* January 13, 1937.

21. Roy L. Smith, *Suburban Christians,* sermon on "Burning Bushes and Burning Hearts," page 105. (Harpers, 1933.)

22. *The Christian Century Pulpit,* January, 1930.

23. Thiselton Mark, *The Pedagogics of Preaching,* page 22.

24. See George Adam Smith, *The Historical Geography of the Holy Land,* Chap. 19.

25. *The Christian Century Pulpit,* April, 1930, page 1.

26. McComb, *Preaching in Theory and Practice,* page 32.

27. Frederick B. Fisher, *Can I Know God?* page 10. (Harpers, 1934.)

CHAPTER V

GATHERING MATERIALS—LITERATURE AS A SOURCE

1. *Larry—Thoughts of Youth,* page 90. (Day, 1931.)

2. M. S. Rice, *Hearing the Unheard,* page 6. (Harpers, 1935.)

3. *Ibid.,* page 34, sermon, "Get Out of My Way."

4. Lynn Harold Hough, *The University of Experience,* page 81. (Harpers, 1933.)

5. Beecher, *Windows for Sermons,* page 16.

6. Arthur Gossip, *The Hero in Thy Soul,* page 119. (Scribners, 1936.)

7. *Ibid.,* page 120.

8. *Ibid.,* page 164.

9. Frederick B. Fisher, *Can I Know God?* page 78, quoting Walt Whitman, *"Leaves of Grass."*

10. Shakespeare, "Cymbeline."

11. Source unknown.

12. Frederick B. Fisher, *Can I Know God?* pages 41, 42, sermon on "Is Christianity True?" (Harpers, 1934.)

13. Halford E. Luccock, *Contemporary American Literature and Religion,* pages 2, 3. (Willett, 1934.)

14. *Ibid.,* pages 156, 157.

15. Lenora Mattingly Weber, "The First Robin," in *Good Housekeeping,* May, 1935.

16. William L. Stidger, *There Are Sermons in Books, That God's House May Be Filled.*

17. S. Parkes Cadman, *Ambassadors of God,* page 288. (Macmillan.)

18. Frederick B. Fisher, *Can I Know God?* pages 42, 43. (Harpers, 1934.)

19. James Black, *The Mystery of Preaching.* (Revell, 1924.)

20. John A. Kern, *The Ministry to the Congregation,* page 223. (Cokesbury.)

Chapter VI

KEEPING MATERIALS

1. John James Ingalls, "Opportunity," quoted in *Quotable Poems,* Clark and Gillespie.

2. James Black, *The Mystery of Preaching,* page 75. (Revell, 1924.)

3. *Ibid.,* page 75.

4. Joseph Fort Newton, *If I Had Only One Sermon to Prepare,* page 197. (Harpers, 1932.)

5. S. M. Berry, *Vital Preaching,* pages 87, 88.

6. Edgar De Witt Jones, *American Preachers of Today,* page 203. (Bobbs-Merrill, 1933.)

7. Joseph Fort Newton, *If I Had Only One Sermon to Prepare,* page 121. (Harpers, 1932.)

8. Edgar De Witt Jones, *American Preachers of Today,* page 237. (Bobbs-Merrill, 1933.)

9. Joseph Fort Newton, *If I Had Only One Sermon to Prepare,* pages 15-158. (Harpers, 1932.)

10. Edgar De Witt Jones, *American Preachers of Today,* page 66. (Bobbs-Merrill, 1933.)

11. Joseph Fort Newton, *If I Had Only One Sermon to Prepare,* page 212. (Harpers, 1932.)

CHAPTER VII

BUILDING ILLUSTRATIONS INTO SERMONS

1. *The Christian Century Pulpit,* April, 1933, pages 1, 2.

2. Lynn Harold Hough, *The University of Experience,* page 41, sermon, "Paradoxes of Living." (Harpers, 1933.)

3. Charles W. Gilkey, *Perspectives,* page 51, sermon, "The Truest Test of Religion." (Harpers, 1933.)

4. Oswald W. S. McCall, *The Gods of Men,* page 15, sermon, "Lone Eagle."

5. Roy L. Smith, *Suburban Christians,* page 42. (Harpers, 1933.)

6. Harry Emerson Fosdick, *The Power to See It Through,* page 40. (Harpers, 1935.)

7. *Ibid.,* page 208.

8. *Ibid.*, page 62.

9. Arthur Gossip, *The Hero in Thy Soul,* page 7. (Scribners, 1936.)

10. John A. Kern, *The Ministry to the Congregation,* page 226. (Cokesbury.)

11. *Ibid.*, page 228.

12. Charles R. Brown, *The Art of Preaching,* page 130.

13. Henry Ward Beecher, *A Treasury of Illustration,* the Introduction.

14. Halford E. Luccock, *Preaching Values in the New Testament,* page 163. (Abingdon, 1928.)

15. M. S. Rice, *Hearing the Unheard,* pages 69, 70, sermon, "Christ's Etiquette." (Harpers, 1935.)

16. Tillett and Nutter, *Hymns and Hymn Writers of the Church,* page 254. (Cokesbury.)

17. *Ibid.*, page 254.

18. John A. Kern, *The Ministry to the Congregation,* page 225. (Cokesbury.)

19. Appeared in *Current History,* January, 1928, and was reprinted in the *Epworth Highroad,* November, 1934.

20. Charles R. Brown, *The Art of Preaching,* page 130. (Macmillan, 1932.)

21. James Black, *The Mystery of Preaching,* page 67. (Revell, 1924.)

22. Frederick B. Fisher, *Can I Know God?* (Harpers, 1934.)

23. Lynn Harold Hough, *The University of Experience,* page 19. (Harpers, 1933.)

24. S. Parkes Cadman, *Ambassadors of God,* page 255. (Macmillan.)

25. Quoted by Gilbert Moods, *The Preacher's Guide,* pages 42, 43.

CHAPTER VIII

COMPOSING THE ILLUSTRATION

1. Lynn Harold Hough, *The University of Experience,* page 8. (Harpers, 1933.)

2. *Ibid.,* page 9.

3. *Ibid.,* page 90.

4. Charles W. Gilkey, *Perspectives,* page 78. (Harpers, 1933.)

5. Allan Knight Chalmers, *Give Me Another Chance.*

6. *Ibid.*

7. Lynn Harold Hough, *The University of Experience,* page 80. (Harpers, 1933.)

8. Ralph W. Sockman, "The Divine at the Door," in *The Christian Century Pulpit,* January, 1930.

9. Ivan Lee Holt, *The Return of Spring to Man's Soul,* page 10. (Harpers, 1934.)

10. Sir Wilfred Grenfell, *Forty Years for Labrador,* page 84. (Hodder, 1934.)

11. Harry Emerson Fosdick, *The Power to See It Through,* pages 43, 44, sermon, "Handicapped Lives." (Harpers, 1935.)

12. Marc Connelly, *The Green Pastures.* Copyright, 1930, and reprinted by permission of the publishers, Farrar and Rinehart, Inc.

13. Clovis Chappell, *Sermons from the Psalms,* page 102, sermon, "The Ageless Theme." (Cokesbury.)

14. Harry Emerson Fosdick, *The Power to See It Through,* pages 39, 40. (Harpers, 1935.)

15. M. S. Rice, *Hearing the Unheard,* pages 81, 82, sermon, "The Expected Perfect." (Harpers, 1935.)

16. *Ibid.,* page 82.

REFERENCES AND NOTES

CHAPTER IX

THE STORY METHOD OF PREACHING

1. Margaret Eggleston, *Fireside Stories,* page xii. (Harpers.)

2. Clovis Chappell, *Sermons from the Psalms,* page 94. (Cokesbury.)

3. Harry Emerson Fosdick, *The Power to See It Through,* page 13, sermon, "Christians in Spite of Everything." (Harpers, 1935.)

4. Charles W. Gilkey, *Perspective,* pages 115, 116, sermon, "The Life Beyond." (Harpers, 1933.)

5. Luke 16: 1-9.

6. Ivan Lee Holt, *The Return of Spring to Man's Soul,* page 1. (Harpers, 1934.)

7. Harry Emerson Fosdick, *The Power to See It Through,* page 42. (Harpers, 1935.)

8. Roy L. Smith, *Suburban Christians,* pages 29, 30. (Harpers, 1933.)

9. Margaret Eggleston, *The Use of the Story in Religious Education,* page 46. (Harpers, 1920.)

10. Oswald W. S. McCall, *The Use of Literature in the Pulpit.*

11. Clark and Gillespie, *Quotable Poems,* in two volumes.

CHAPTER X

THE ART OF EFFECTIVE PRESENTATION

1. Harold A. Prichard, *The Minister, the Method, and the Message,* Chap. 5.

2. *Ibid.,* page 151.

3. J. Edgar Park, *The Miracle of Preaching,* page 142.

271

Chapter XI

THE SOUL OF THE BUILDER

1. Edgar De Witt Jones, *American Preachers of Today*, page 307. (Bobbs-Merrill, 1933.)

2. *The Christian Herald*, June, 1937.

3. Father Abram J. Ryan, "The Valley of Silence."

4. Irving Babbitt, *Rousseau and Romanticism*, page 291, quoting *Artist and Public*, page 134. (Houghton Mifflin, 1919.) I have taken the liberty to invert the description of the two artists as originally portrayed.

5. J. Edgar Park, *The Miracle of Preaching*, page 90.

6. R. S. Smith, *Preaching as a Fine Art*, page 24.

7. William De Witt Hyde.